Siân Evans was born and br
Her plays have been performec
BBC Radio and in theatres in V
and she has produced episodes
and 'Peak Practice' (ITV). Her ___ ___ _____
'Hereafter' will be broadcast on ITV in 2001.

Othniel Smith was born in Newcastle-under-
Lyme in 1962, and has lived in Cardiff since his
university days, where he gained a degree in
psychology. He has had a number of plays and short
stories broadcast on BBC Radio. He is currently
studying for an Open University M.A. in
Humanities, and hopes one day to earn a living.

Roger Williams has written plays for theatre
companies including Made In Wales and The
Sherman Theatre Company; television for BBC2,
HTV and S4C; and radio for BBC Radio Wales and
BBC Radio Cymru. In 1998-99 he was playwright-
in-residence at Sydney Theatre Company and the
Australian National Playwrights' Centre. In 2000 he
was awarded a Playwright's Bursary by the Arts
Council of Wales. He lives in West Wales.

PARTHIAN BOOKS

New Welsh Drama II

Little Sister

Siân Evans

Giant Steps

Othniel Smith

Killing Kangaroos

Roger Williams

Edited by Jeff Teare

PARTHIAN BOOKS

First published in 2001.
All rights reserved.
Parthian Books
53 Colum Road
Cardiff
CF10 3EF
www.parthianbooks.co.uk

ISBN 1-902638-13-1

Published with financial support from the Arts Council
of Wales.

Typeset in Galliard by NW.

Printed and bound by ColourBooks, Dublin, Ireland.

With support from the Parthian Collective.

Cover: Cribyn by Sarah Snazell
© Estate of Sarah Snazell.
Private collection, with thanks to Mrs V. MacDonald.

A CIP catalogue record for this book is available from
the British Library.

'No art; no letters; no society.'

Thomas Hobbes

Contents

Art Against the Odds

In my introduction to the first volume of 'New Welsh Drama'('98)
I wrote, 'The writers have all gone on to write other things and
Made In Wales survives to fight another day.' Well, Lewis Davies
and Roger Williams have certainly written other things and Afshan
Malik has developed both her writing and scientific career. Made
In Wales, on the other hand, has had its main funding from the
Arts Council of Wales (ACW) withdrawn. ACW admitted that
Made In Wales's work was 'held in high regard' but they
nevertheless decided to cut their support to new writing in Wales
by over one third and, for reasons never explained, insisted on
there being only one designated new writing company in Wales,
working both in English and Welsh, for less money. (Made In
Wales had been set up in 1982 to develop and produce work in
English, Dalier Sylw some years later, to work in Welsh). When I
started work in Cardiff in 1995 there were seven small ACW
funded companies (not including those working in TIE) doing
what I considered to be interesting work in and around Wales's
capital city. Now (September 2000) there are, to my knowledge,
two. I have no idea why this is the case. You'll have to ask ACW
(Museum Place, Cardiff, CF10 3NX).

However, on to the plays...

'Little Sister' by Siân Evans was, like 'Safar' in Volume I, part of our 'Three Plays By Women' Season of 1996. (And I sincerely hope that the third play, 'Sea That Blazed' by Christine Watkins, also gets published one day). It was a commission that I inherited from my predecessor, Gilly Adams. She warned me that it was 'unfinished'. In fact, it was hardly started. Still, at least this enabled Siân and myself to work together on developing the play. My main contribution to this process was, quite properly in my dramaturgical opinion, structural, but I well remember some distinctly uncomfortable discussions, to me as the male director at least, on the play's subject matter. The relationship between director and writer on a new play is often tricky and I pay tribute to Siân for her professionalism and patience through what was potentially an especially difficult process. (I should also add, as an historical note, that Siân was, in 1996, the first writer ever to bring a laptop computer into a rehearsal of mine).

Rehearsing the rape scene was one of the most difficult things I've done in thirty years of working in British theatre. (After one rehearsal I remember deciding that the best thing for us all to do was go for a walk and have an ice cream.) 'All power' (as we used to say) to Brendan and Lowri for the way they performed it. In fact, I have to say, that Lowri's performance in this play is one of the best things it's ever been my privilege to be involved with. I'd also like to pay tribute to Sue Mayes for a stunning set and to James Westaway (God rest his soul) and Shiv Grewal for one of the best stage kisses, ever! Perhaps my strongest memory of the whole production was having to ask one audience to, at least, adjourn to the pub next door, as their ad hoc (and somewhat heated) after-show discussion was delaying our locking-up of the theatre.

'Giant Steps' by Othniel Smith was very much part of my attempt to give Made In Wales' work a multi-cultural perspective. The first thing I did with the Company in 1995 was to set up a multi-cultural writers workshop and my first actual production with Made In Wales was a show-case of these writers' work.

How large a task I had set myself was soon revealed by a

phone call to ACW. By 'multi-cultural' they assumed I meant 'Welsh and English speaking'. When I explained that I was mainly talking about Welsh writers from non-European backgrounds I was met with a long silence. In fact, it was only possible to stage 'Giant Steps' because of a special grant from the London Arts Board to promote Black and Asian writing. The snag was, we had to open in London. So, the entire Made In Wales production team decamped to Brixton (at exactly the same time as Ron Davies as it happens, but I know nothing, honest...).

Thanks to old mates from Stratford East, we were made very welcome at Oval House in Kennington, and found a great lighting designer in their resident techie, Crin. It has to be said that the London press had a bit of a problem with a 'Black' play from Wales, but, perhaps not as much of a problem as some of the white Cardiff audience had with a 'Black' Welsh play (as opposed to a Welsh play with one or two black characters). Despite our previous two productions at Chapter in Cardiff ('Gulp' and 'My Piece Of Happiness') averaging over 90% capacity, 'Giant Steps' only achieved about 16%. However, the production got the best set of reviews of any MIW show that I was responsible for (Time Out called it 'inspirational') and, at least towards the end of the run at Chapter, I saw more black faces in the audience than at any other theatre production I'd been to (outside of a school) in Wales, since 'Safar'. Abiding memories? Farimang's appearance as Oliver's ghost in a costume given to him by his own father, Aileen discovering the anger in her character in one late rehearsal (I thought she'd broken the hospital bed), Peter's impressions of both Farimang's and Aileen's performances (lovingly intended, of course) and the tears on the faces of two middle-aged black woman after a performance at Oval House.

'Killing Kangaroos' had a much longer gestation period than the marsupial itself. After the huge success of his first MIW production, 'Gulp', Roger and I had a number of conversations as to what his next commission should be. Roger was keen on a boy-band musical, I wasn't. Then he mentioned his Welsh speaking

Australian relations...

It took me about six months to get a deal together to get him to Australia to research and write the play. It then took about another nine months for the play to be workshop-presented at the Australian National Playwrights Festival in Canberra. Back home it took, all in all, over a year to get six dates for the show (that's performances not venues) in Wales. Finally, 'Kangas' went very well in Cardiff, Newport and Swansea. One reviewer thought we'd targeted an under twenty-five audience too successfully (does she know how difficult this is?) and another only grudgingly admitted that 'the audience loved it' but, finally (after we'd closed), two other reviewers did pay tribute to Roger's skill as a playwright, the social acuity of his play and the fun of the production as a whole. 'Good on' the fantastic cast (who says Oz soap stars can't act?), designer, technical crew, and, especially, the 'fabulous beyond' Acting ASM!

My main memory of this production has to be from Newport (well, my mum came from Newport). We were doing an 'intention run' to remind the actors why their characters were going on and off stage (it's quite complicated). I asked Valmai, who was looking a trifle perplexed on one entrance, 'What do you want?' 'Fish and chips!' came the resounding reply. (Mind you, Shelley's swimming pool exit in the technical rehearsal comes a close second, but you had to be there...).

So, three more new Welsh plays to be read, studied and hopefully performed. At the time of writing, although currently unfunded by the Arts Council of Wales, Made In Wales still exists (madein.wales@virgin.net), all three writers featured in this volume are definitely writing other things and this director, at least, lives to fight another day (and is available for work - have pencil, will travel). I'd like to take this opportunity to thank all the people who worked on the twenty-odd (OK, some odder than others) shows put on by Made In Wales in my time, especially Rebecca Gould, who (as she never tired of telling me) did most of the work really. The audiences who supported us deserve credit as well, especially those brave souls who accepted the offer of an outdoor performance in March (it's a long story). And lastly, heartfelt thanks to my long-suffering partner Susie, who has sat through most of the hundred-and-twenty or so productions I've thus far perpetrated on the, thankfully still stoical, British public.

Finally, to whom it may concern: - the writers, actors, directors, designers, stage-managers and technicians still attempting to work in Welsh theatre deserve a better level of organisational and financial support than they are currently getting. There's an awful lot of creative talent in Wales, but it must be nurtured and encouraged if Wales is to have a creative as well as an economically viable future. Forcing these people to become economic migrants (most of them currently have to go to London) is a disaster for the development of a vibrant, Welsh performing arts culture for the future. And, anyway, I need them to be here and successful to support me in my no-doubt impecunious dotage!

Cheers,

Jeff Teare

Ex-Artistic Director, Made in Wales
September 2000

LITTLE SISTER

SIÂN EVANS

Little Sister was premiered by Made In Wales at The Point, Cardiff Bay, as part of their 'Three Plays By Women' Season in September 1996, with the following cast:

Lisa	Lowri Mae
Martin	James Westaway
John	Brendan Charleston
Helen	Shireen Shah
Man/Colin	Shiv Grewal

Directed by	Jeff Teare
Designed by	Sue Mayes
Lighting by	Dennis Charles
Stage Manager	Sally Wozencroft
Assistant Director	Rebecca Gould
Assistant Designer	Kate Lynham

UNLESS STAGE DIRECTIONS STATE OTHERWISE, ACTION IS CONTINUOUS.

SCENE 1 IS SET IN THE PRESENT DAY. SCENES 15 AND 16 FOLLOW ON FROM THIS SCENE. SCENES 2 TO 14 BEGIN SEVEN YEARS BEFORE AND ARE IN SEQUENCE. SCENE 17, THE EPILOGUE, IS CHRONOLOGICALLY THE FIRST SCENE.

SCENE 1

A hostess club in Cardiff in present day.

The club is upmarket and high-tech. There are several images of young girls scattered around the club.

The time is 2 a.m. The club is empty apart from a woman in her late thirties who is clearing up behind the bar.

A younger woman, Lisa, walks past, ignoring her. She approaches a man who is sitting alone at one of the tables.

LISA: What are you doing here?

JOHN: I came to pick you up.

LISA: You don't usually.

JOHN: It's raining.

LISA: When is it not raining? I'd have got a cab.

JOHN: I thought we could have a chat.

LISA: Couldn't it wait?

JOHN: Don't get a chance. You're asleep when I leave and
               I'm asleep when you come home.

LISA: That's what being successful means. It means never
               having to talk. Look, I should be helping clear up.

JOHN: It's not your job to clear up. I never cleared up. It
               gives the wrong message.

*Lisa sits down at the table next to John. From time to time her eyes
skim the room as she keeps an eye on proceedings.*

LISA: Let's talk in the car.

JOHN: You always fall asleep.

LISA: True.

JOHN: Have a drink.

LISA: No thanks.

John beckons the woman behind the bar over.

JOHN: Fetch us two glasses of white wine there's a love.

(To Lisa)

You can fall asleep anywhere. You never have any trouble sleeping.

LISA: Clear conscience.

JOHN: Sleep of the innocent.

The woman returns with two glasses of wine, bangs them down on the table and walks off. Lisa glares at her.

LISA: I'll talk to her later.

JOHN: She told me you've given her the sack.

LISA: She's pregnant.

JOHN: Helen's been here a long time - she's very good at her job.

LISA: What do you want me to do? Give her maternity leave?

JOHN: She's been here longer than you.

LISA: So?

JOHN: You know she lost her job at the university as well.

LISA: What's that got to do with me? Anyway that was years ago. Why the sudden interest in Helen's career?

JOHN: I was just wondering how she'll support herself and the kid.

LISA: She shouldn't have left it so late.

JOHN: She's been trying for years.

LISA: How do you know?

JOHN: She told me. I've known her a long time. Some of the girls become part of ...a sort of family.

LISA: Some family!

JOHN: And I'm just wondering what she's going to do with a kid and no job.

LISA: If she's got any sense she'll have put something by for a rainy day. Anyway her parents are rich, aren't they? They'll come to the rescue.

JOHN: Is that what you've done?

LISA: What?

JOHN: Put something by...... for a rainy day?

LISA: None of your business.

JOHN: It was my business.

LISA: And now it's *our* business it's making a profit.

JOHN: I know. You've transformed this place. And me.

LISA: Too right I did.

PAUSE

JOHN: Things have changed. My life has changed.

LISA: You wouldn't have a life if it weren't for me.

JOHN: Exactly. And I'm very grateful. That's partly the reason why I wanted to talk to you.

LISA: You don't have to give me anything. I've got everything I want.

PAUSE. Helen walks past carrying a tray with a bottle of champagne and two glasses.

JOHN: I hope she has put something by...

LISA: She's 37. She couldn't have done this job for much longer anyway...

JOHN: She's a smart woman.

LISA: That's got nothing to do with it. You should know that. We don't employ smart women - we employ girls. I'm surprised she's lasted this long. I must be getting sentimental in my old age.

JOHN: All twenty three years of it. You and she used to be quite friendly.

LISA: Did we? We had nothing in common. Apart from being here. She's always said she wanted a kid and now she's got one. She should be happy. It's a good excuse for her to leave. She'll get another job, in another college. She'll write up her thesis. She'll make up with mummy and daddy. Her father's a merchant banker isn't he?

JOHN: I know.

LISA: I forgot. You know everything.

PAUSE

JOHN: Your friend rang earlier. Colin.

LISA: Rang where?

JOHN: Here.

LISA: I thought you meant he rang home.

JOHN: Did you give him our number?

LISA: Of course not. That's why I was surprised. You weren't here.

JOHN: Helen told me. Asked me to pass the message on.

LISA: Which was?

JOHN: He can't make tomorrow. *(He looks at his watch)* I suppose I mean today.

LISA: What a shame! I'll have to go shopping instead.

JOHN: I didn't realise he was still coming.

LISA: He's a loyal little soul.

JOHN: Obviously. You hadn't mentioned him for ages so I
                thought you'd had enough of him. Told him to get
                lost.

LISA: Why should I do that?

JOHN: You said he was weird.

LISA: Did I? I must have got used to it. There's a lot
                weirder people than Colin around.

LISA: I bumped into Martin earlier on. In town.

JOHN: All right is he?

LISA: He may have to shut up shop.

JOHN: It's not his to shut is it?

LISA: They own it between them.

JOHN: Bad location. They were too upmarket. Most
                people round here wouldn't know what a sun-dried
                tomato was if it hit them in the face. They're like
                that though aren't they?

LISA: Who are?

JOHN: You know. Them. They've got to be exotic. They can't just do fish and chips. Run a cafe. It's got to be avocados and pecan pie.

LISA: They're still together.

JOHN: I suppose they are.

LISA: And happy.

JOHN: Good for them.

LISA: I once told him it wouldn't last.

PAUSE.

JOHN: Shall I lock up?

LISA: I'll do it. I got the books back yesterday. Takings were up 40% this year.

JOHN: That's good.

LISA: Good? It's brilliant. There are places opening and closing within weeks round here!

We're doing brilliantly. When the money's tight, what do men do? Do they think of their wife and kids? Do they take care of their pennies? Do they hell! They panic. They blow it all in a night. Sod the wife, sod the kids. And we're laughing all the way to the bank. I don't feel sorry for them. If it weren't us it'd be the pub or the betting shop or scratch cards.

40%!

JOHN: Is it always about money?

LISA: The poor is hated even of his own neighbour, but the rich hath many friends.

JOHN: You still remember all that?

LISA: It surfaces from time to time. Can we go home now? I just want to sleep.

JOHN: I haven't asked you yet.

LISA: Asked me what?

JOHN: What I came to ask you.

LISA: I thought you just came to pick me up because it's raining.

JOHN: I think we should get married.

LISA: *(stunned)* What?

JOHN: I want us to get married.

LISA: Why?

JOHN: Why not? After seven years-

LISA: No.

JOHN: We live together, we work together, we sleep together ... we might as well be married.

LISA: No. How could you think that I...

JOHN: O.K, forget it...

LISA: How could you imagine that I ... I can't believe you just asked me that.. I know you. I know what you are. Jesus! Then you'll be asking me to start a family. Let's have a baby, a little boy, a little girl. A little girl ...

JOHN: All right! Leave it! Leave it!

PAUSE

JOHN: Look, I'm sorry. Maybe I shouldn't have asked.

LISA: I'll forget it. As soon as I get into bed and fall asleep I'll forget it . Thank God I sleep so well. It's a blessing. I can blot out everything.

SCENE 2. SUMMER SEVEN YEARS BEFORE.

Martin is getting ready to go out. He is alone in the flat.

MARTIN:.   He has dark hair, dark straight hair, a piece falls into his eyes. Dark eyes. Not jet black, not so black that you can't see the pupil. Brown, syrup brown. Olive skin, of course. Slim but not puny. Tall? My height enough. He'll dress ... very casual ... he's not interested in clothes. An Italian not interested in clothes, get real! This one isn't. Just jeans and a T-shirt. An old T-shirt. His mouth, not thin, not too full, soft. He's a mechanic, no, a stone mason...A stone mason! Where did that come from? A fisherman? A student? He doesn't speak any English. I have to learn Italian ... we don't need to talk of course because we're too busy ... we can use sign language and my Italian. We'll spend the afternoons together, the siesta. In cool dark rooms where the shutters filter out the light and heat. Drowsy afternoons on white sheets, feet on marble floors...

Under a streetlight two men are kissing. One of the men is Martin. The other is in his late twenties. He's slightly scruffy and has taken off his jacket and tie. There's a briefcase near his feet.

MAN: That aftershave!

MARTIN: It's not ... I'm working in a perfume factory, for the summer ...

MAN: Is that what it is?

MARTIN: It's terrible this weather. It clings to your sweat.

MAN: Don't worry, I can breathe through my mouth ...

MARTIN: I wanted to ask you something.

MAN: Bloody hell! What now?

MARTIN: A favour.

MAN: What?

MARTIN: It's difficult...to say..

MAN: *(worried)* What is?

MARTIN: Could you..?

MAN: What?

MARTIN: Could you do an accent?

MAN: *(relieved)* What kind of accent?

MARTIN: Italian.

MAN: English with an Italian accent or Italian?

MARTIN: Do you speak Italian?

MAN: No.

MARTIN: So why did you say Italian like that - like you could speak it?

MAN: I mean I can bluff.

MARTIN: How?

MAN: You know. La donna e mobile! Spaghetti! Cappuccino..

MARTIN: Your accent's lousy.

MAN: That's Italian with an English accent.

MARTIN: Just forget it.

MAN: I've got a friend who's Italian. He's Welsh but his family are Italian - he speaks it anyway.

MARTIN: So?

MAN: I could ask him to come along and talk in Italian while we fuck.

MARTIN: Why don't I just cut out the middleman and fuck him instead?

MAN: You could do both. I don't care. Why do you have to be so bloody picky? It's only a fantasy. It's not real.

MARTIN: He's fluent is he?

MAN: I dunno. *(pause)* You want me to give him a ring, now?

MARTIN: Would you?

MAN: You think I'm stupid? You expect me to stand around here like a lemon waiting for bloody Giancarlo to arrive.

MARTIN: Giancarlo?

MAN: That's very good, that accent.

MARTIN: I've been practising, with a tape.

PAUSE

MAN: I'm not in the mood anymore. I'd better be going. My shepherds pie will have dried up, and I've got work in the morning. I'm sorry... Look...

He fishes around in his jacket for a scrap of paper and a pen.

Here you are.. Giancarlo Fecci.
His parents run a fish and chip shop in Roath.

MARTIN: Oh.

MAN: What did you expect? That his dad runs La Scala
                and his mother's Sophia Loren?
                What else would they be doing living in Cardiff?

He hands Martin the paper.

                See you round.
                Ciao.

*He holds out his hand quite formally. Martin shakes it. Martin looks
at the piece of paper in his hand. He folds it very carefully and puts it
into his pocket.*

SCENE 3

John and Martin's flat. Lisa has cooked dinner.

JOHN: So how come if you're such good friends I haven't
                seen you before?
                Come to think of it I haven't seen many of Martin's
                friends. One might be forgiven for thinking he
                didn't have any!

MARTIN: Very funny.

LISA: Everyone liked Martin, at school.

JOHN: Did they?

MARTIN: I'm a popular guy!

JOHN: Well I never. – He just doesn't want to bring them back here in case they meet me?

MARTIN: I left my oldest friends behind in Whitchurch.

JOHN: It's not exactly Guatemala, is it? You can still see them Martin.

MARTIN: I do.

JOHN: Good. You've more chance of seeing them than your mother after all.

MARTIN: Don't start on about her.

JOHN: I wasn't. Really. I hope she's enjoying Warrington.

MARTIN: Wolverhampton.

JOHN: Of course you'd know after your many visits. That was a delicious meal Lisa. Who taught you to cook?

LISA: I learnt at school.

JOHN: Not at mother's knee?

MARTIN: Lisa's mother's dead.

LISA: When I was born.

JOHN: That must have been terrible.

LISA: I don't remember it.

JOHN: No, I mean growing up without a mother.

He puts his hand briefly on Lisa's arm. Martin watches. Lisa stands up and collects the plates, and takes them into the kitchen.

MARTIN: Don't wash them Lisa, I'll do it later.

Martin looks at his watch.

JOHN: What's the matter?

MARTIN: Nothing.

JOHN: Not nothing. She's a nice girl.

MARTIN: That's right.

JOHN: Not your type, I wouldn't have thought.

MARTIN: And you'd know what that is would you?

JOHN: I just didn't think she was your type - I thought
               you'd go for someone ...different.

MARTIN: She's a friend.

JOHN: Of course she is.

MARTIN: Why do you always have to-

JOHN: Always have to what?

Lisa comes back in.

LISA: I've got some ice-cream if you'd like it.

JOHN: I LOVE ice-cream.

MARTIN: I don't think we've got time.

JOHN: Are you going out?

MARTIN: Pictures.

Lisa doesn't know about this.

JOHN: *(to Lisa)* What's on?

MARTIN: Some American crap.

JOHN: Romance isn't dead then. I bet he won't even pay
               Lisa. I bet he won't even buy you a bag of chips on
               the way home.

MARTIN: And all because the lady loves....

JOHN: What's wrong with that? I bet Lisa wouldn't say no
               to a box of chocolates.

LISA: I don't eat much chocolate.

JOHN: You don't need to diet.

LISA: I'm not on a diet.

JOHN: She's perfect, isn't she Martin?

LISA: It's very kind of you to let me stay here Mr Harris.

JOHN: Don't worry about it. You can stay as long as you
               like. Martin's told me what happened and I'm really
               sorry. People shouldn't have kids if they don't want
               to take the rough with the smooth.

Martin snorts at this. John ignores him. Lisa is drawn in.

You think he'd be proud of such a lovely daughter. He should be supporting you through a difficult time, not throwing you onto the street. Anyway, as far as I'm concerned you're a mature young woman; you can come and go as you please. Remind me to get a key cut for Lisa.

LISA: It's only temporary . As soon as I find a job...

JOHN: I said don't worry about it. I know how hard it is to find work, part of the reason I started my own business. Martin's been lucky - he stinks to high heaven but...

MARTIN: It's a crap job.

JOHN: It's better than nothing. What sort of thing would you like to do?

MARTIN: I'm checking out the factory. I shouldn't think it'll be too difficult. At least finding a summer job...

LISA: *(replying to John)* I'm not sure. I can type and I can work a switchboard...

JOHN: I might be able to find you something

MARTIN: Lisa's not done that kind of work before-

LISA: What kind of work?

MARTIN: You've not even done any waitressing have you?

JOHN: You don't even know what I'm going to say?

MARTIN: You're talking about the club.

Martin gets up and puts on his coat.

JOHN: Debbie, the receptionist, left last Tuesday and we
                haven't replaced her yet.

LISA: Reception work isn't that...

MARTIN: I just don't think Lisa would fit in and anyway she's
                too young.

Martin gives Lisa her coat, he's hurrying her.

JOHN: It was just an idea. I'll keep my mouth shut. I wish
                you every luck in your job hunting Lisa.

LISA: Thank you.

JOHN: Hold on Martin.

John fishes around in his pocket.

LISA: *(whispers to Martin)* What's the matter?

JOHN: You won't have been paid yet. Here.

He hands Martin a £20 note.
Martin takes the money reluctantly.

LISA: Martin, aren't you going to say thank you?

MARTIN: For what? He owes me a lot more than this.

Martin puts the money in his back pocket.

JOHN: Forget it Lisa. His mother never taught him any manners.

John ruffles Lisa's hair. They smile at one another.

                Have fun.

SCENE 4.

THE CLUB.

Helen has a middle-class English accent. This is a spiel she's reeled off many times before.

HELEN: You've met John, obviously. That was Mal on the door and Gabby in reception. I'm Helen and I'm head hostess. Have you ever been in a club like this before?

LISA: No

HELEN: They pay the entry fee at the door. £5 if they're a member, £10 if not. Yearly membership is £100. They come in and they go straight to the bar. It's your job to approach the customer and persuade him to sit at a table with you. To sit at the table with you is £40, this includes the first bottle of champagne. You get half of the forty pounds. After that you get £5 for every bottle under £100 or £15 for every bottle over £100. Your goal is to get them to drink as many bottles as you can. This means that you also have to drink the stuff. You can try and get rid of it but if you're caught it doesn't look good. So you have to be able to hold your drink. You are over eighteen aren't you? You keep all the tips. Some are as little as a tenner, some as high as fifty. You want a regular punter who will come back and ask for you.

We're a very friendly bunch. Some of the girls are actresses, some are dancers, singers, some are students - I'm an academic, I'm just finishing my thesis. I think its healthier if you have a life outside, otherwise it becomes your life.

If the customers refuse to pay or get stroppy then John or Mal will help out. Likewise if they touch you or become offensive in any way. Of course some are just deeply offensive people. That happens, that's just their personality, they don't mean to be rude but they just are deeply offensive by nature - they probably won't do anything. Japanese tend to spend a lot and keep their distance physically though they may talk dirty. Arabs don't tend to treat us with enormous respect. Germans, French, Dutch usually want a bit of sleaze. Americans and English, by which I mean English and Welsh, are usually more concerned about their wallets. If they start playing up or saying they don't have the cash then tell them we accept all credit cards.

And if you're ever caught with your fingers in the metaphorical till you're out the door.
Understood?

Oh yes. If a customer asks you to go home with

him what will you say?

LISA: Sorry? I don't understand.

HELEN: If a customer asks you to go home with him.

LISA: I'd say no!

HELEN: Good, that's what we want to hear. If they become insistent then say you're on your period. The rest of the time you just have to be inventive. If you want to string them along that's up to you. As I said you make most of your money from your regulars.

If you do decide you'd like to 'socialise' with any of the customers then you must make that arrangement outside, off the premises. Is that clear?

How old did you say you were?

LISA: *(hesitates)* Eighteen.

HELEN: And one other thing.

LISA: What's that?

HELEN: Smile.

Lisa smiles. Helen stares at her. Lisa gives a bigger smile.

HELEN: Wonderful!

SCENE 5

JOHN'S FLAT. EVENING.

John is sitting in a chair reading the paper, he is wearing his coat. Lisa is getting ready to go to the club. She wanders in and out, once in a towel, once in a dress. She is drying her hair, putting on make-up, etc.

LISA: I won't be much longer.

JOHN: No rush. Plenty of time. I just thought I'd go down a bit earlier tonight. I've got accounts to do and I keep putting it off. Martin out is he?

LISA: Just gone to the chippie.

JOHN: Across the road?

LISA: He said something about Roath.

JOHN: What's he want to go all the way to Roath for a chippie?

LISA: Maybe it's a very good one.

John puts down the paper. He watches her while she puts on her make-up; she's humming quietly.

JOHN: You seem to be settling in with the other girls.

LISA: They're not what you expect - actresses and dancers and students.

John gets up and stands behind her.

LISA: Some of them have got real glamour. How does this look?

JOHN: Gorgeous.

LISA: I'm not used to wearing makeup. Dad wouldn't let me.
                  Not even perfume. 'Perfume is for street girls...'
                  Does it make me look fat this dress?

JOHN: No. Just a little bit cuddly.

John puts his arms around her and cuddles her. She turns around. He kisses the top of her head.

LISA: Thank you.

JOHN: What for?

LISA: For giving me a job. And letting me stay here.

JOHN: Don't be silly.

LISA: I'll pay you back.

JOHN: Will you now!

LISA: I'm going to try and save.

JOHN: Wait and see how you get on. It doesn't suit everyone. You might want to do something else.

LISA: I'm just glad to have a job. I know people who left school two years ago and have never had a job.

JOHN: They can't have tried very hard.

LISA: Dad hasn't rung has he?

JOHN: Not that I know of.

LISA: I thought he might cool down after a bit and want to know how I'm getting on.

JOHN: I'd forget about him. He doesn't deserve a
              daughter like you.

*John cuddles her. Lisa shifts uncomfortably but John holds her tight
and she settles in and starts to enjoy the cuddle.*

JOHN: Is that nice?

LISA: Mmn.

Lisa snuggles in.

JOHN: What a little baby you are. What a cuddly little
              baby.

*Lisa giggles. He strokes her hair. His movements are slow and strong.
He kisses her. She's embarrassed and tries to break away. She suddenly
realises that his grip is extremely tight. The progression from affection
to aggression is very smooth.*

He puts his hand on her breast.

LISA: Please don't.

JOHN: Women treat me like shit. You're not like the
              others. You're kind. Other women couldn't give a
              shit. You're so soft.

He lifts up her dress.

JOHN: You touch something inside me Lisa. I don't want
to hurt you. I love you. This is out of love. Don't
worry no-one will find out. I won't hurt you.
Be still. Be a good girl now.
I won't hurt you.

If it hurts a little that's good isn't it?
A little hurt is good isn't it?
It makes it better. That's what they tell me.

I love you. I do this out of love.

He rapes her. It is very brief.

Lisa cries.

What are you crying for?
There's no need to cry.

He hugs her again and tries to comfort her.

I'm sorry.

You are very special. You're so sweet, there's no
helping it.

I never want to hurt you. Do you believe me?

Lisa looks at him but doesn't answer. Pause. He smoothes her hair.

I should get going really. Why don't you take the
evening off? Do you have a headache?
You don't look too well.
Why don't you have an early night? I'll tell Helen.
Saturday's a quiet night anyway.
Will you do that?

Lisa nods.

JOHN: You don't have to... I just thought...

LISA: I'll stay.

JOHN: Good girl.

*John kisses her on the cheek. He leaves. Lisa sits quietly in a chair.
She stays there without moving. Eventually she begins to clean the
make-up off her face.*

She hears a voice from the hallway.

MARTIN: *(singing)* When the moon hits your eye like a big
pizza pie that's Amore!

When the world seems to shine like you've had too
much wine that's Amore!

Martin bursts in and sings to Lisa.

Bells will ring ding a ling a ling, ding a ling a ling
and you'll sing Vita Bella!
Hearts will play tippy tippy tay, tippy tippy tay like a
gay tarantella - Lucky fella...

What's wrong with you?

LISA: Nothing... You seem happy

MARTIN: Happy? Happy! What an inadequate little word that
is to describe my...bliss..my euphoria ..my..

LISA: Who is it?

MARTIN: *(savouring the name)* Giancarlo Fecci

LISA: He's Italian then.

MARTIN: No, Czech! It's the real thing Lisa. For the first
time I've tasted the real thing.

LISA: And how does it taste?

MARTIN: It tastes very nice.

LISA: Only nice?

MARTIN: I thought you might show a flicker of interest, a scrap of pleasure that your best friend has found true love.

                Aren't you meant to be working tonight?

LISA: I've got the evening off.

MARTIN: Saturday night! That's very generous of him. Of course, there's no business men on Saturday, they've all gone back home.

LISA: I've got a headache.

MARTIN: Shit! It's Saturday night!

LISA: So?

MARTIN: I was meant to be baby sitting tonight.

LISA: Baby sitting who?

MARTIN: Stella, a neighbour's kid. Shit! I'll ring in the morning and grovel.

LISA: You had other things on your mind, obviously.

MARTIN: Look Lisa - I'm sorry it's worked out like this.

LISA: Like what?

MARTIN: I know you wanted a job but..

LISA: What?

MARTIN: I'm saying, what am I saying? I'm saying it can't be much fun. All those greasy men pawing you.

LISA: They're not allowed to paw.

MARTIN: Mentally pawing, they can mentally paw.

LISA: So do men in the street..

MARTIN: Yeah but you don't have to sit with them all evening and laugh at their jokes.

LISA: It's a job and it's better than no job. I can cope.

MARTIN: You've only been there a couple of weeks and you hardly seem to be having a good time, that's all.

LISA: Since when did you care that I was having a good time?

MARTIN: Oh dear!

LISA: I asked you if there was anything going at your place but you forgot to ask....didn't you?

MARTIN: I did!

LISA: Well did you help me get another job? When I told you John had offered me this job did you say 'Don't take it Lisa, I'll help you find something else' ?

MARTIN: Look Lisa I'm doing my best. First you turn up on my doorstep homeless! That's O.K. I may not have seen you for months but what are friends for? I don't mind. My dad says it's O.K you can stay - rent free - for as long as you like...within a couple of days he finds you a job...it's not the greatest job in the world..but there are worse..

Look, Giancarlo is going to start his own business..if it gets going maybe he can take you on..

LISA: I won't hold my breath.

MARTIN: For God's sake Lisa! Stop feeling sorry for yourself!

Start looking for other jobs. Dad's not going to throw you out. You can put up with him for a bit longer, he's not that bad!

Pause

LISA: I think I'm going out with your father.

MARTIN: What? Don't be daft... Are you serious? That's a bloody stupid thing to do isn't it!

LISA: Why?

MARTIN: Because you're 16 and he's 40.

LISA: So?

MARTIN: It's your life. Who am I to tell you what to do?

LISA: You said it. What's his name? Giancarlo? It won't last.

MARTIN: How so?

LISA: It's not real. You just wanted someone Italian. I feel sorry for him. It's a fantasy isn't it?

MARTIN: And what do you know about fantasy Lisa? Fantasy requires a bit of imagination, a bit of subtlety...

LISA: Which I haven't got is that what you're saying?

MARTIN: Let's not row Lisa. I was in a really good mood
when I came in.

LISA: I'm sorry I spoilt your mood.

MARTIN: So am I. You haven't asked me about my results.

LISA: Have you got them?

MARTIN: I failed. Art. I passed history. How can you fail Art?

LISA: I'm sorry.

Martin hugs Lisa. Lisa tries not to cry.

MARTIN: It's not that much of a tragedy! I can resit! Anyway
who needs Art when you have a lover!

LISA: Martin.

MARTIN: What?

LISA: I am happy for you... Let's go out. Let's go out and
celebrate. Let's go out and get drunk.

SCENE 6

THE CLUB

Helen and Lisa are having a drink together.

HELEN: The worst was when she started drinking in the park, in public. No wonder my father left her. When they threatened to put me into care she cleaned up her act for a while. She never stopped telling me about the sacrifices she'd made to bring me up - her brilliant acting career! A career! A couple of walk-ons in Z Cars. Of course if it hadn't been for me she would have been the next Vanessa Redgrave! She used to say I was never like a child, I was always an old woman. Not surprising really. I must have taken one look at her and thought this upbringing's going to be a DIY job. Having menopausal males wittering in your ear all evening is nothing, not when you've had an alcoholic mother unloading onto you day and night for eighteen years...

LISA: My mother died when I was born.

HELEN: Mine might as well have done for all the mothering I got... So how come you're sixteen and going out with a 40 year old club owner?

LISA: It just happened. I'm a friend of his son Martin.

HELEN: The invisible son.

LISA: This kind of place isn't his scene.

HELEN: What happened to you last Saturday by the way?

LISA: I had a headache. John said it was O.K to take the night off.

Helen shrugs.

HELEN: You said you wanted to ask me something.

LISA: I know I've only been working here a few weeks but...I'm not making as much as I thought I would. I wanted to save money, to get a place of my own.

HELEN: Does John know that?

LISA: No.

PAUSE

LISA: Why are you working here?

HELEN: Money. The job at the university is only a few hours
                a week.

LISA: You don't like it do you?

HELEN: It's O.K.

LISA: No, I mean you really don't like it. I don't love it,
                but you seem to hate them.

HELEN: Hate who?

LISA: Them. The men.

HELEN: Do I? Does it show that much? I smile all the time.

LISA: That makes it even more obvious.

Helen laughs

HELEN: I suppose you could say I hold them in contempt.
                Not all of them. Most.

LISA: Then why do you do it if you hate it that much?

HELEN: I told you, I need the money.

LISA: But with your qualifications you could get another
job.

HELEN: What is this?

LISA: Sorry. It's just that I don't like it, but I have
nothing else. If I had a choice I wouldn't do it.

HELEN: There's always choice.

LISA: Is there? Then you're choosing to do it.

HELEN: For the time being, yes. Maybe you're right. Maybe
it is perverse.
Maybe I enjoy watching men make complete pratts
of themselves. I have something they want and I'm
not going to give it to them.

LISA: Have you ever... gone out with any of them?

HELEN: Once. He was quite a wealthy guy.

LISA: He paid you.

HELEN: It was a one-off.

PAUSE

LISA: Does anyone else do that?

HELEN: I don't ask.

LISA: Did John know?

HELEN: He knows everything.

LISA: What did he say?

HELEN: Not a lot. It's none of his business really.

LISA: But if he didn't like it he could sack you.

HELEN: He wouldn't. It's not so easy finding good staff. Why are you asking me all this?

LISA: Just curious.

HELEN: Really? Well, I had no regrets. I recarpeted the flat and updated my PC...
              You don't need money do you?

LISA: I don't want to rely on him.

HELEN: I can understand that. He's crazy about you.

LISA: Is he?

HELEN: Don't you realise?

LISA: I didn't ask for it, it's not as if I asked for him to feel like that.

HELEN: I didn't say you did.

LISA: Sorry.

HELEN: Aren't you attracted to him?

LISA: No. A little.

HELEN: He's a powerful man. I don't mean..what is usually meant by that word...materially powerful. He has a force, of personality. He's what we'd call in the jargon an unreconstructed male.

LISA: A what?

HELEN: A man's man. He enjoys being in control of people rather than things. He's not even bothered by money, except as a means to an end.

LISA: Do you think he's attractive?

HELEN: He has something.

LISA: I don't know why he's interested in me.

HELEN: Don't you?

LISA: Do you?

HELEN: You distract him. From the world. You're sweet.

LISA: *(laughing)* Sweet?

HELEN: And for him the sweetest thing is that you don't even realise it.

LISA: Would you help me?

HELEN: If I can.

LISA: I need to make some money.

HELEN: Are you asking me to find you a client?

LISA: Yes.

HELEN: Just one?

LISA: Yes.

HELEN: You're not going to make a lot of money with just one.

LISA: But you just said you bought all those things..

HELEN: Yes but I saw him every week for a year.

LISA: Couldn't I find someone like that?

HELEN: You can try.

LISA: How much..how much would it be..could I expect.

HELEN: £150 maybe...I don't see why not.

LISA: £150.

HELEN: It's not bad for half an hours work. Depends how often. There was someone in on Saturday - friend of a friend. He was asking but he wanted someone very young. Still, you don't look eighteen.

LISA: Maybe it's not such a good idea. Forget it.

HELEN: It's up to you.

SCENE 7

THE FLAT 1989.

Martin is packing things into a bag. He hears a noise and stops. His father walks in. He goes to the kitchen and comes back with a beer. He sits down and puts on the telly. He rewinds the video and presses play. The familiar sounds of an international rugby game.

MARTIN: Have you heard the news?

JOHN: What's that?

MARTIN: Have you heard what's happened? About Stella...

JOHN: Yeah. Terrible thing. Terrible.

Martin does up the bag. John sees it but ignores it.
MARTIN: I hate this place. It stinks.

JOHN: You should do the washing up more often.

MARTIN: I mean this estate.

JOHN: I don't suppose anyone loves living here. Do you?

MARTIN: You're home early.

JOHN: Quiet night. I'll go back down later to close up. She was a nice kid.

MARTIN: She was brilliant.

JOHN: You knew her quite well didn't you?

MARTIN: I knew the whole family.

JOHN: They might want to interview you.

MARTIN: They might.

JOHN: Don't look so scared. They're probably not looking outside the family.

MARTIN: What do you mean?

JOHN: It's usually in the family.

MARTIN: What?

JOHN: They usually start the investigation in the family. If there wasn't a sex motive. If that's the case you can be 80% certain it was one of the parents.

MARTIN: How do you know that?

JOHN: A copper, a customer at the club told me. Was it a sex attack as well?

MARTIN: I don't know... I don't know.

An exciting moment in the game; John lifts himself out of the chair and falls back into it in disappointment.

So how's Lisa getting on?

JOHN: Really well. She's not as shy as you think. She's reserved. That's nice. She gives the place a bit of tone. Her and Helen.

MARTIN: Have you got her working yet?

JOHN: My girls are not working girls.

MARTIN: Really!

JOHN: If they make private arrangements that's their business. What do you think I am!

MARTIN: I don't know what you are.

PAUSE

JOHN: Going somewhere?

MARTIN: I'm starting a business

JOHN: What tonight?

MARTIN: Of course not tonight.

JOHN: A business. Where?

MARTIN: In town.

JOHN: On your own?

MARTIN: No

JOHN: Who with then?

MARTIN: A guy.

John stops watching the game momentarily.

JOHN: What 'guy'?

MARTIN: A guy I met.

JOHN: Where?

MARTIN: I don't remember...in a pub.

JOHN: What pub?

MARTIN: The Anchor.

JOHN: Where's that?

MARTIN: Down by the docks.

JOHN: You go down to the docks for a drink?

MARTIN: Sometimes, after I've been to the gym.

JOHN: What sort of business?

MARTIN: Sandwich bar.

JOHN: Oh, big time then!

MARTIN: Yeah, big time!

JOHN: Who is he? This guy you met in a pub, down in the docks?

MARTIN: He's Italian. His family are Italian.

JOHN: Their business is it?

MARTIN: Was. He's taking it over. It was a cafe, but it wasn't
                doing too well. He's.. we're going to do it up.

JOHN: Why you?

MARTIN: What?

JOHN: You've not got any experience in business and you
                can't make a sandwich to save your life. Why should
                he pick you?

MARTIN: He trusts me.

JOHN: More fool him!

MARTIN: There's a flat above the cafe. He says I can use it.
                Live in the flat above the business. It's more
                convenient.

JOHN: Of course. And where does he live?

No answer

JOHN: So when are you moving out?

MARTIN: Now.

JOHN: I see. What about Lisa?

MARTIN: Lisa?

JOHN: Don't you care? She's your girlfriend.

MARTIN: My girlfriend? Would you like that? Would you like to be screwing my girlfriend?

JOHN: What?

MARTIN: I'm surprised that you've taken up with her at all-

JOHN: You're talking rubbish.

MARTIN: She's a little too old for you isn't she? Sixteen's getting rather mature for your taste isn't it?

John hits him.

JOHN: At least they're girls, at least they're women! Do you think I'm stupid? Do you think I don't know what you do? What you are?

John sits back down and picks up his drink, he stares at the telly. Slowly Martin gets up.

You might as well take all your stuff.

MARTIN: I've got all I need. You can keep the rest, throw it
in the bin, burn it.

*His nose is bleeding. The commentator's voice rises in pitch.
Martin glances at the screen.*

MARTIN: God I hate that fucking game.

*John doesn't move. The televsion commentary continues to rise and
fall. Martin leaves.*

JOHN *(without turning to look at Martin)*: I guess we're all a bit
upset tonight.

John hears the door shut and turns around.

JOHN: Shit! Shit!

SCENE 8

A TINY ROOM WITH LITTLE MORE THAN A BED IN IT.

*Lisa sits on the edge of the bed. A man in his late thirties sits on a
chair near the bed. He is immaculately dressed. Neither of them
speaks. Every now and then she glances up at him but he doesn't move.*

She looks at the clock.

LISA: It's been a beautiful day. I don't notice usually because there are no windows in the club. No windows and no clocks. Then people don't realise how long they've been in there. They don't realise it's seven o'clock in the morning. Are you not feeling well? Would you like a cup of tea?

The man - 'Colin' - stares at her.

Or something to eat? Would you like something to eat?

Colin shakes his head.

LISA: Did you have to come far? Have you been travelling a long way? I thought maybe you had to travel in your job. Driving can be really tiring. I don't drive myself but I know other people who do..

COLIN: I don't drive.

Silence

COLIN: I suppose I should sort out the..financial arrangement.

He takes out his wallet. He removes a credit card and hands it to her. She looks at it.

LISA: I don't have the...thing... to... the machine... I don't have one...

He takes back the card.

COLIN: Sorry.

He fishes about for the cash.

COLIN: It was seventy-five wasn't it?

LISA: What?

COLIN: Isn't that it? Seventy five pounds.

LISA: *(embarrassed)* I was told more.

COLIN: More?

LISA: Yes.

COLIN: How much more?

LISA: A hundred and fifty.

COLIN: A hundred and fifty! There must be a mistake.

LISA: Yes, there must be.

COLIN: A hundred and fifty! I don't understand.

LISA: Helen told me that.

COLIN: Who's Helen?

LISA: Your friend Helen.

COLIN: It doesn't make sense.

LISA: I know.

COLIN: I'm sorry but a hundred and fifty, I can't do that.

LISA: O.K.

COLIN: Would ninety do?

LISA: I...

COLIN: A hundred?

LISA: Yes...yes O.K. that's fine.

He hands over the notes and she takes them awkwardly, not knowing where to put them. She puts them down on a small table. She begins to undress, again awkwardly.

COLIN: Don't. There's no need. I wanted to say
                  something...

PAUSE

                  I'll tell you my name. It's Colin...
                  But I don't want you to ask anything else.
                  And please don't tell me about yourself either. It
                  doesn't matter. Do you understand?

LISA: It's up to you.

COLIN: Good.

LISA: I was just trying to make conversation.

COLIN: I know.

LISA: I thought you might be feeling, uncomfortable.

COLIN: I'm fine.

LISA: Good. What you want to do?

PAUSE

COLIN: I'd like to play a game.

LISA: *(a little frightened)* What sort of game?

COLIN: Hide and seek.

LISA: *(PAUSE)* Hide and seek? How do you mean?

COLIN: You hide and I'll look for you.

LISA: You mean real Hide and Seek.

COLIN: Yes!

LISA: There's nowhere much to hide in here.

COLIN: Doesn't matter. Use your imagination. Pretend. Close your eyes. Like children do. They close their eyes and think they're invisible.

LISA: Alright. I'll try. Turn around then.

COLIN: I'll count to a hundred.

LISA: I think twenty'll do.

COLIN: One, two, three..

Lisa gets up slowly, looking about for somewhere to hide. She crouches down next to the bed and closes her eyes. She's still plainly visible.

LISA: Ready.

COLIN: Fifteen,   sixteen,   seventeen,   eighteen, nineteen...twenty!

He stands up and turns around. He pretends he can't see Lisa.

COLIN: I'm coming! I'm coming to find you! Where are you?

He looks under the bed, beneath the bedclothes, on top of the wardrobe, in every corner. Then he 'sees' her and pretends to creep up on her. He 'catches' her.

COLIN: Got you!

LISA: Ah!

LISA LAUGHS. COLIN TICKLES HER. LISA LAUGHS EVEN MORE. SHE STILL HAS HER EYES CLOSED. THIS GOES ON FOR A SHORT WHILE THEN HE STOPS. SHE OPENS HER EYES. THEY ARE BOTH BREATHLESS. SHE IS GIGGLING. THEN SHE TICKLES HIM. HE JUMPS UP

AND SHE CHASES HIM AROUND THE ROOM. SHE
CATCHES HIM, THIS TIME HE HOLDS HER IN A BEAR
HUG AND WON'T LET GO. LISA IS SURPRISED, THEN
SHE TRIES TO BREAK FREE. IT TAKES A LITTLE WHILE,
HE EVENTUALLY RELEASES HER. HE LOOKS AS
THOUGH HE MIGHT BURST INTO TEARS.

HE RECOVERS THEN PICKS UP HIS COAT.

LISA: You're going?

COLIN: It's eight o'clock. I've got to get back.

LISA: So?

COLIN: I'll ring and arrange another time. A month today?
              Would that be convenient for you?

LISA: Yes...I suppose so.

COLIN: Goodnight.

HE LEAVES. LISA LIES BACK ON THE BED AND LAUGHS
WITH RELIEF.

SCENE 9

Lisa is lying in bed. John is sitting next to her. Lisa is watching a nature video.

John turns off the video.

LISA: I was watching that!

JOHN: You watch those bloody things all the time. It's like living in one of those menage a trois - me, you and bloody David Attenborough.

LISA: They're educational.

JOHN: What? So you're going to be a zoologist in your next life!

LISA: You don't have to have a reason to improve yourself... What's the matter?

JOHN: I don't know. I do. Someone rang for you.

LISA: Rang here?

JOHN: No, at the club. I was given a message. It was about a room.

LISA: A room?

JOHN: Yes, a room. You'd arranged to go and look at a room.

LISA: Did I?

JOHN: Lisa!

LISA: Oh that room! I was curious. I was wondering how much a room cost.

JOHN: I need you here.

LISA: I'm not going anywhere.

JOHN: That's why you're looking for rooms.

LISA: Even if I did rent a room, we could still go out together. You'd still see me everyday at the club. I'd spend the weekends here.

JOHN: Then what's the bloody point in moving out?

LISA: I'm not saying I am moving out. It was just an idea.

JOHN: We get on well, we have fun don't we?

LISA: I'm not moving out.

JOHN: Good.

LISA: Is that all that's the matter?

John is silent. He sits on the edge of the bed. Lisa kneels behind him and puts her arms around his neck.

JOHN: How long is this going to last eh?

LISA: What are you talking about?

JOHN: Five years? Ten?

LISA: Why do you think like that? I don't.

JOHN: I don't like to think about it but I have to. In ten years time you'll be twenty seven and I'll be fifty....

LISA: So what?

JOHN: Do you think you'll still be here?

LISA: *(PAUSE)* Yes.

JOHN: Really?

LISA: Yes!

JOHN: Why?

LISA: You've been kind to me.

JOHN: Gratitude!

LISA: No.

JOHN: I've not always been kind to you.

LISA: You didn't mean it. John, what's the matter?

JOHN: I've got to tell you something and when I've told you you'll want to leave me.

LISA: Don't be daft.

JOHN: I'm not being daft, it's true.

LISA: I won't leave you.

JOHN: Promise?

LISA: Promise.

JOHN: I love you Lisa.

He hugs her. We see his face, Lisa doesn't.

LISA: I love you too. Now tell me.

PAUSE

JOHN: I just wanted to kiss her.

LISA: Who?

JOHN: Just a kiss... She had this defiant look, as though she
              was stronger than me. Her! Stronger than me!
              That's what did it really. It was so ludicrous it made
              me mad. And it rose from my feet, from the earth
              beneath my feet and pushed its way up, up into my
              body, my arms, my hands, my mouth. I shouted
              too. I think I did. She fought back. She was strong,
              surprisingly strong for such a slight build.

LISA: You're talking about that girl Stella aren't you?

LIsa takes her arms from around his neck and sits back.

JOHN: It came from a kind of arrogance I suppose. That
              she wasn't afraid. I hated that. I couldn't tolerate it.
              Who did she think she was? To shout at me? To
              swear at me? A child like that to show no respect
              towards a grown man. She wasn't so innocent as
              you might think, so sweet and innocent. The
              language she came out with! Unbelievable!

All for a little kiss! Maybe more, who knows - that would've been up to her.

Why did she have to be so arrogant? Why couldn't she concede with good grace? What was it to her, a kiss? She had hundreds of them, thousands of them stored up, she could've given them away freely, to anyone, to me. What was so terrible about me? Am I so repulsive?

I wasn't asking the impossible. Just an arm round my neck and her soft cheek against mine, her arm, trusting around my neck... what did she think I was going to do?

Where did she learn that language? At 13 - fucking this and fucking that, it was disgusting, unseemly, perverted. A child shouting that kind of abuse at me. No-one has any respect, any fear of anyone anymore - without force. As soon as I hit her she stopped shouting, stopped shouting that foul language. There was blood on her mouth. I kissed it at last. But she didn't put her arm trusting around my neck...

He sighs

LISA: Why are you telling me this?

JOHN: Because I need you here. You're good Lisa. You have goodness.

LISA: What would you do if I went to the police?

JOHN: What could I do? Nothing. I'm at your mercy. I'm
               telling you because I trust you.
               Because you have enough goodness for both of us.
               You have to believe me too when I say I didn't
               mean to hurt her. You do believe me, don't you?
               You won't answer. You see I told you. I told you
               you'd want to leave me.

LISA: I didn't say that.

JOHN: I can see it in your face.

LISA: I wasn't.... Why her?

JOHN: I was afraid. Afraid of losing you. I knew you would
               go sooner or later. I guess I took it out on her. She
               was a provocative little thing. She was always
               smiling at me...
               I thought it would heal me. Like this film. The old
               man who makes a liquor out of children's hearts.
               He has to gouge out the hearts of two virgins - a
               boy and a girl. It's his only hope of survival. He
               does it but one dose is never enough. His victims
               follow him everywhere, warning other children,
               pulling back their shirts to show everyone the dark

hole where their hearts had been.

He moves to touch Lisa. She jumps.

JOHN: Don't worry. It will never happen again.

He strokes her hair.

>Are you afraid? Have I frightened you?
>There's no need to be afraid. I'd do anything for
>you Lisa. As long as you stay here with me you can
>do what you like. I'll give you anything you want.
>I'm in your hands Lisa.

He kisses Lisa. She is too frightened to move. Blackout.

SCENE 10

Lisa and Martin are in the park.
Martin is munching his way through a huge elaborate French roll.

MARTIN: You can't imagine how it makes you feel in control.
                In control of your life, your destiny. I thought it
                was all crap, that small business shit, but it's a kind
                of freedom. After all these years of doing what I'm
                told, it is freedom. No-one gives a damn whether
                I'm straight or gay - they only care about my

money, Lisa. It sounds naff but I have 'power' at last.

You want to be really independent? Forget education, forget grovelling to some employer - find a gap in the market and exploit it.

Here do you want some of this? It's too much for me.

Lisa shakes her head.

LISA: Funny to think of you being a businessman - like your father.

MARTIN: I wouldn't call dad a businessman. Dad's not motivated enough.

He only started it to get access to the girls. He never encouraged business because he wanted them all to himself. That club will never fulfil its potential.

Lisa shivers.

MARTIN: What is it?

LISA: Do you feel cold?

MARTIN: No, not particularly. That's a nice jacket. Making a bit more money now?

LISA: A bit.

MARTIN: I told you it would get better.

LISA: How's Giancarlo?

MARTIN: He's very well. His Italian is terrible by the way. We
              go to evening classes together.

LISA: I'm sorry John hit you. He told me.

MARTIN: Why was it your fault? Did you tell him to hit me?
              It was going to happen sooner or later.

LISA: Had he ever hit you before?

MARTIN: No. He's not like that.

LISA: Isn't he?

MARTIN: What's the matter?

LISA: I'm not sleeping very well.

MARTIN: Why's that?

LISA: Not since you moved out. I miss you.

MARTIN: I miss you too, but I just couldn't stay. It wasn't just about me and dad.

I couldn't bear to be reminded of Stella every time I came home. Every time I walked down the stairs. I couldn't pass their flat and see her window. See the Children In Need stickers and the bloody fluffy toys.

LISA: I've been having nightmares.

MARTIN: Have you?

LISA: I see her. Stella.

MARTIN: I didn't think it would affect you the same way.

How's dad coping?

LISA: He said she wasn't an angel.

MARTIN: What the fuck does that mean? She's not an angel! Does that mean she deserved to be beaten to death? God he's bloody weird sometimes.

LISA: Martin.

MARTIN: What?

LISA: Your dad.

MARTIN: What about him?

LISA: You don't think he might have had something to do with it?

MARTIN: What? Stella's murder? Lisa!

LISA: I don't mean that he meant to kill her but he might have you know, approached her...

MARTIN: What kind of crazy stuff is this?

LISA: You told me once he used to bring girls back to the flat.

MARTIN: Did I?

LISA: How old were they?

MARTIN: I don't know. I was asleep most of the time. They were probably girls working in the club and they're all over 18.

LISA: Like me.

MARTIN: Lisa! This is my father we're talking about. He may be a homophobic jerk but he's not a murderer.

LISA: I'm sorry.

MARTIN: So am I. It's bad enough having a friend murdered without someone coming and telling you your father did it.

LISA: I didn't say he did it.

MARTIN: That's what you're implying.

LISA: It's just a couple of things he's said.

MARTIN: Like what?

LISA: Forget it.

MARTIN: If you really have suspicions then go to the police. Personally I think it's a load of crap.
Anyway I heard they've picked someone up.

LISA: Have they?

MARTIN: That's what I heard. Look I've got to get back. This is our busy time and Giancarlo's covering for me. We're working all the hours god made. If there's any justice in this world we'll be in the black by Christmas.

LISA: Wealth gotten by vanity shall be diminished; but he that gathereth by labour shall increase.

MARTIN: Something like that.

LISA: Well, thank you for your valuable time.

MARTIN: Lisa! I'm sorry. Maybe I over-reacted... But you can't expect me to take you seriously, can you?

LISA: I'll see you round.

Martin grabs her arm, she shakes him off and walks away.

MARTIN: Lisa!

SCENE 11

Lisa is lying in bed asleep, with John. She sits up. She 'sees' a girl at the foot of the bed.

GIRL: I'm very cold Lisa. Kiss me Lisa, kiss me. Please, I'm very cold. I'm so cold. No-one told me it would be so cold and I want to be warm again. I

91

want to go home Lisa, I want to go home to my
mother and father, my brothers and sisters. I'm not
bad Lisa. I'm only a little girl. Don't be frightened
of me. Please hold me. Please. Keep me warm.
Please.

Lisa whimpers with fright.

GIRL: You still have a heart Lisa. He's taken my heart.

*She stops whining suddenly and is very angry. Her voice is different,
deeper, more mature.*

GIRL: THAT FUCKING BASTARD HAS TAKEN MY
                 HEART. GIVE IT BACK TO ME YOU
                 BASTARD! CUNT! FUCKER!

*Lisa is screaming now. John wakes up and turns on the light. The girl
has disappeared. John comforts Lisa.*

JOHN: Ssh! Ssh! Just another bad dream sweetheart.
                 It's just another of those bad dreams.

SCENE 12

THE CLUB.
It's the early hours of the morning. Lisa is rifling through a cupboard.
Helen comes in unexpectedly and surprises her.

LISA: I thought everyone had gone home.

HELEN: I was upstairs making a call. I came back down to lock up.

LISA: Don't worry. I'll do it. You can go if you like.

HELEN: Have you got keys then?

LISA: Yes.

HELEN: For the safe as well?

LISA: Yes.

HELEN: Since when?

LISA: Since Tuesday. John didn't tell you?

HELEN: No he didn't!

LISA: Does it matter?

HELEN: The security in this place is a shambles already. It doesn't help if he gives out keys to all and sundry.

LISA: I think it's only me. But I agree security is bad.

HELEN: Were you looking for something?

LISA: The books. John asked me to bring them home.
            The accountant's calling round on Monday and he
            wants to have a quick look over them.

HELEN: I see.

LISA: I was curious. I was wondering how much profit
            this place made.

HELEN: Are you interested in business? Or are you looking
            after your interests?

LISA: They're not my interests, they're John's and yes I
            am interested in business.

HELEN: I'm sorry, I had no idea.

LISA: Something someone said to me. About this place
            not realising its potential... That new club, the one
            in Newport, it belongs to a friend of John. Have
            you ever been there? It's packed. Every night. They
            must be making a fortune. I was thinking about it

last night in bed. They've got blown up paintings on the wall. This place looks really tatty. It's needs doing up.

HELEN: Try telling John that.

LISA: I already have.

HELEN: And what did he say?

LISA: He'll think about it.

HELEN: He won't.

LISA: I'll persuade him.

HELEN: I don't think John's that interested in running this place anymore.

LISA: He's a fool not to make the most of it.

HELEN: He gets what he wants from it and that's not necessarily money.

LISA: The girls you mean. He's slept with everyone in here hasn't he?

HELEN: Pretty much.

LISA: And everyone who will come to work here.

HELEN: I don't know. He's never lived with anyone before,
           not since I've known him.

LISA: The girls in this place in Newport were smart. But
           young. None of them looked more than twenty.

HELEN: And they were doing well?

LISA: Packing them in.

HELEN: Fresh meat.

LISA: If that's what they want then that's what we have to
           give them.

HELEN: Market forces.

PAUSE

LISA: You know. I think we could run this place better
           than John.

HELEN: What us? You and me?

LISA: Why not?

HELEN: I haven't got the time.

LISA: I thought you were only doing a few hours teaching a week.

HELEN: At the moment. Once I've finished my thesis I expect to get more.

LISA: I thought they didn't have any money, colleges. Someone's always on the news complaining about cut backs and that.

HELEN: But there's always room for the best.

LISA: And that's you is it?

HELEN: I like to think so, yes. It's a competitive world. Even for academics. Especially for academics. You have to be positive. This is a sideline for me. A day job.
               As a career! It's never entered my head.
               And what do you do Helen?
               (She impersonates Lisa) I run a hostess club love..

She laughs

LISA: Why not?

She stops laughing

HELEN: Have you found a room yet?

LISA: No. I haven't looked for a while. Last place I went
to was a student house.
The carpet was so swollen with damp you couldn't
get the door over it.
Slug trails all over the kitchen.

HELEN: Ugh!

LISA: No point in taking any old dump just for the sake
of it.

HELEN: Depends how desperate you are.

PAUSE

Lisa yawns and rubs her eyes.

HELEN: You look shattered.

LISA: I am.

HELEN: I'm not surprised. You haven't had a night off for
weeks. Is he paying you overtime?

LISA: I'm not complaining. All labour is profit.

HELEN: John was moaning to me. He said he hardly sees you.
                Has something happened?

LISA: Like what?

HELEN: I've no idea. I thought maybe you'd had a row, you were avoiding him.

LISA: No. I like working. I'm not sleeping that's all.

HELEN: I can give you some sleeping tablets if you want.

LISA: Could you?

HELEN: No problem. I'll bring them in tomorrow.

Lisa gathers up the books in her arms and leaves Helen.

SCENE 13

Colin and Lisa's room.

*Lisa is wearing a gingham dress and a white blindfold. She and
Colin are playing Blind Man's Buff. Lisa enters into the spirit of the
game, and seems to be enjoying it as much as Colin.*
*Eventually she catches him and holds him tight. She takes off her
blindfold. They kiss.*
*Colin breaks it off. When they separate we see that the kiss has moved
Lisa.*

COLIN: I'm sorry.

LISA: It's O.K.

COLIN: It was an accident.

LISA: I didn't mind.

COLIN: I should've asked.

LISA: Most people don't.

COLIN: I suppose not.

LISA: It was nice.

COLIN: Your dress is undone. Let me do it up.

*She sits in front of him and he does up her dress. He rests his hands
lightly on her shoulders.*

I dreamt about you last night.

LISA: Did you?

COLIN: And it was you, no-one else.

LISA: Was it a nice dream?

COLIN: I don't remember all of it. I think so.

LISA: Colin. I look forward to seeing you.

COLIN: ,Same here.

LISA: I mean, I really look forward to seeing you.

Colin removes his hands from her shoudlers.

COLIN: Lisa. These are very particular circumstances. It's very easy to become confused.
Do you understand what I'm saying?

LISA: No.

COLIN: It's very easy to lose control of one's feelings.

LISA: I haven't lost control.

COLIN: Good.

LISA: What I meant was, it's very different for me. This time with you, in this room. It's away from everything else in my life. It's cut off from everything. I feel very *(searches for word)* safe here.

COLIN: *(PAUSE)* So do I.

LISA: I feel I can breathe. I feel me. Not what other people want me to be.

COLIN: I'm glad.

LISA: Why won't you tell me about yourself? Just one thing.

COLIN: No.

LISA: Just one little thing? Your favourite colour.

COLIN: Blue.

LISA: Favourite animal.

COLIN: Dog.

LISA: Favourite place.

COLIN: Barry Island.

LISA: You're lying.

COLIN: I am. Liguria, in Italy. We went there on holiday
             when I was a child. The whole family.

LISA: We went to Porthcawl. My auntie had a caravan
             there. It was magic.
             On the whole I'm glad it's over, childhood.

COLIN: Are you?

LISA: Always having to do what other people tell you. My
             dad -

COLIN: Lisa! Don't. Don't bring other people in. Don't
             bring the rest of the world in.

LISA: If that's what you want. It's your money.

SCENE 14

THE FLAT.

Same setting as Scene 11, but instead of Lisa lying next to John, it's Helen. John gets out of bed and walks across the room. He picks up an orange and starts peeling it with a knife.

JOHN: It just needs to be controlled. That's all. It controls me and all my trouble stems from this one thing. If only I could control it. I might have done anything with my life.

One teacher at school told me I had potential. You have tremendous potential John.

I will never go anywhere, be anything unless I can control it. It runs away. It is outside my power. And yet it gives me a feeling of power. For an instant, for a second.

He stands in front of a mirror

I hate myself. No I don't. I hate this thing hanging down in front of me. I hate how it makes me feel. Because I don't always want to feel it do I?

I can control what I feel up here *(tapping his head)* but I can't control that thing.

It comes from the adrenal glands. Some young guy in the States, he operated on himself; he tried to cut out his adrenal glands. He read up on it in the library and then he got the equipment and he opened himself up.

He draws a line across his stomach with the knife

Three hours he searched around inside his guts, he knew they were tucked away behind the liver somewhere. Then the local anaesthetic he'd given himself started to wear off and he had to ring for an ambulance. They were really pissed off with him at the hospital. He was always doing it and they always had to stitch him up again. Imagine. Imagine being that bloody desperate.

Helen cuts in.

HELEN: Please! Spare me the details! Anyway, this is different. I asked you. You're doing me a favour.

JOHN: I'm not sure I want to be a father again.

HELEN: You won't be. A parent, that is. You're not the only person who's helping me out.
And I've made it clear to everyone that all responsibility ends at conception.

JOHN: I see. How long before you'll know?

HELEN: Depends... on how easy it is for me to conceive and how fertile the men are. The rest I can plan.

JOHN: Aren't you scared of bringing it up alone?

HELEN: No.

JOHN: You're very single minded. Independent. I've
            always admired you.

HELEN: From a distance.

JOHN: Well, that kind of behaviour doesn't make you the
            most ... approachable of people.

HELEN: The men in the club don't seem to have that
            problem.

JOHN: That's different.

HELEN: I'm glad you agreed.

JOHN: Anything to help out a friend.

HELEN: It is something I want very much.

JOHN: How will you manage?

HELEN: I'll manage. I went to see a friend last week. I'd lost
            touch with her and then I'd heard she had a baby
            and I used it as an excuse to go and see her. Or the

other way round. I wasn't interested in her, I wanted to hold the baby. He was asleep in the bedroom so I went in and lay next to him. Have you ever smelt a baby's breath? Have you ever felt a baby's breath on your face?

And the way they look at you. They think you're wonderful. They think you're a god just for giving them a drink of milk.

Does Lisa want kids?

JOHN: We've never talked about it. If she did, I'd go along with it. I don't want to lose her.

HELEN: Is that why you've made her manageress?

JOHN: That was her suggestion not mine. I didn't think you'd mind. You're about to leave aren't you? So you keep saying. I thought you could train her up before you go.

HELEN: The department's made me redundant.

JOHN: Have they?

HELEN: That's one of the reasons I want the baby. It would fit in well.

She holds her belly

Funny to think my future might lie in here. That it will transform my life. Which is what I want. I want to be transformed.

JOHN: You make it sound religious.

HELEN: Maybe it is.

JOHN: And if it doesn't happen?

PAUSE

HELEN: So Lisa becoming manageress has nothing to do with the punters.

JOHN: How do you mean?

HELEN: You're not jealous?

JOHN: No.

HELEN: Not even of her friend?

JOHN: What friend?

HELEN: Her client. Don't you know about him?

JOHN: Oh him! Of course I know about him. He asked
me before he asked you.
I recommended her too.

Helen is shocked.

HELEN: Why?

JOHN: Don't worry - he's harmless. A bit weird but
harmless.

HELEN: And if he's not?

PAUSE

JOHN: She's never complained to me. Has she complained
to you?

HELEN: No. She said everything was fine.

Helen begins to dress

JOHN: So, when do you want to try again?

HELEN: See how it goes. I imagine it won't be for a while.
I'll let you know.

SCENE 15

Lisa and Colin's room.
Lisa is out of breath.

LISA: So what happened? You left a message to say you
           weren't coming today. I wish you wouldn't do this.
           I'd made other plans and it's ballsed up my day.

COLIN: I'm sorry.

LISA: If you want to change times or days that doesn't
           matter but giving me half an hour's notice -

COLIN: It's the last time.

LISA: What?

COLIN: I shan't be coming any more.

LISA: Why ?

COLIN: I'm moving.

LISA: So?

COLIN: To Canada. I've got a brother there. He's fixed me
           up with a job.

LISA: You weren't going to turn up today were you?

COLIN: No.

LISA: Then why did you? You don't mind my asking you a question ? If this is the last time I'm going to see you.

COLIN: I felt I owed you something.

LISA: Really?

COLIN: Of course. You must have seen, noticed that... there's a difference.

LISA: Yes.

COLIN: I'm not the same. I'm much... happier.

LISA: Good.

COLIN: And I'm very grateful.

They sit in silence for a while.

LISA: Canada.

COLIN: Yes.

LISA: That's the first piece of information you've given me about yourself, apart from your name.

COLIN: I know nothing about you either. We agreed that -

LISA: You agreed that -

COLIN: From the start.

LISA: At least you know where I work. What do you do? It can't matter now you're leaving the country.

COLIN: I'm a tax inspector.

LISA: Is that it? I thought you must work for M15 !

COLIN: Nothing so exotic!

LISA: Are you married?

COLIN: No. There's very little about me that's interesting. I live in the same house in which I was born.

LISA: You've never asked me anything.

COLIN: Like what?

LISA: I don't know. Anything about me, my life.

COLIN: It doesn't mean I don't know you.

LISA: That's not the point. I do have another life and that's where I spend most of my time, not in this room with you.

COLIN: O.K

He tries to think of something to ask her.

What did you do before you worked at the club?

LISA: Nothing.

COLIN: Nothing?

LISA: I was at school.

COLIN: You were very young weren't you?

LISA: Don't I look it?

COLIN: *(hesitates)* Yes.

LISA: I feel ancient.

COLIN: You have a lovely face.

LISA: Do you really think so?

COLIN: I've always thought so. Especially when you laugh.

LISA: Not very often then. Do you ever think about me, did you, outside this room?

COLIN: No, not a lot. I didn't want to.

LISA: Why?

COLIN: You're very unhappy. I didn't want to think about that. You seemed to be less and less happy. And I was feeling better and better. Are you disappointed I'm leaving?

LISA: Yes.

COLIN: I'm flattered.

LISA: I've got used to you.

COLIN: Used to my weirdness.

LISA: I didn't say that.

COLIN: No, but you must have thought it. I'm sorry I haven't talked to you; there was too much going on in here *(he taps his head)*.

LISA: I might have helped.

COLIN: You did. I'm sorry I couldn't help you.

LISA: Why? Do I need help?

COLIN: Probably not. Not now.

LISA: No, you're right. Not now. I'm not so naive now.

COLIN: Naive?

LISA: Innocent.

COLIN: What do you mean by that?

LISA: I didn't know anything.

COLIN: Ignorant.

LISA: More.

COLIN: What?

LISA: Trusting.

COLIN: And that trust has been betrayed?

LISA: Yes.

COLIN: When did you realise?

LISA: A long time ago.

COLIN: And was it the first time?

LISA: *(thinking)* No.

COLIN: Then why was it different?

LISA: Because, because it was deliberate. It didn't just
           happen. It wasn't accidental. He knew he was using
           me and he didn't care.

COLIN: And what did you do?

LISA: What do you mean?

COLIN: Did you do something to stop him using you, or
           did you accept it?

Lisa is silent

COLIN: I'm just saying that it's not because something happens, but because you accepted it. Whatever 'it' is. That's what changed you. It's easier to accept and not trust anyone ever again.

To say everyone is the same, so why shouldn't I accept this man who uses me because all other men will use me. Trust is not something you lose, like your keys or your wallet.

Anyway you haven't lost it. You trusted me. I was a stranger and I asked you to do strange things but you still trusted me.

LISA: And haven't you used me too?

LONG PAUSE.

COLIN: Have you gained nothing? Apart from money of course, I'm not referring to the money.

LISA: When you said you felt better... What did you mean...How?

COLIN: You want to know.

LISA: Yes. I want to know. You owe me that.

COLIN: Sally. My little sister Sally.

PAUSE

LISA: Go on.

COLIN: Well. We, Sally and I, we'd been playing out in the street, all day, all evening.

It was one of those long summer days when it stays light until at least nine.

We'd been having a grass fight. The council had cut the grass and they'd left it lying around as usual.

The smell of cut grass. Sally loved it...

This evening all the other kids must have already gone in. Only Sal and I were left.

Our eyes had got used to the dusk, the dim light.

If she'd been on her own then mum and dad might have been concerned but of course I was there - to protect her.

It's still very clear. She was wearing a dark blue T-shirt and white shorts and flip flops. The flip flops were old and worn and the bit between the toe kept coming out of its socket. I had to pop it back in for her every now and again.

We were playing hide and seek and I was counting.

I'd got to 87. I always insisted on counting up to a hundred. It used to drive her crazy. We were such complete opposites. She was totally wild, fearless and I was so.. cautious, obssessed with order.... neatness.

At 87 I heard a noise. I thought, shall I turn around? No. I'll get to a hundred first. The noise got louder and louder. I heard my name. I heard her shout my name and I thought she's cheating! She's knows I haven't reached a hundred yet! 97, 98. There was a scream and a thud. 100.

The car had vanished. I thought she was messing around. I went up to her and prodded her with my foot. Come on Sal! Her flip flops were off and I picked them up - they'd come unstuck again. She didn't move and I wanted to laugh. I pulled her over, she was lying face down. She wasn't marked on one side but when I turned her over the impact had dislodged one of her eyes. She was dead of course. The other eye was almost closed but this one lay sparkling against her cheek and I so wanted to put it back. It was untidy.

She was 9. Two years younger than me. Now she's thirty years younger than me.

LONG PAUSE

It's not what you were expecting is it?

LISA: No.

PAUSE

COLIN: I didn't think about her for years. And then one day
               I woke up and I couldn't stop thinking about her.

LISA: And now?

COLIN: It's much easier.

He takes out his cheque book

LISA: Don't, please. Not today.

COLIN: You're right.

He embraces her awkwardly.

He looks at her and then kisses her.

COLIN: I'm glad you're not Sally anymore.

LISA: It didn't stop you sleeping with me.

Colin is silent.

LISA: John asked me to marry him this morning.

COLIN: And what did you say?

LISA: I said no.

COLIN: But you won't leave him will you?

LISA: I might.

COLIN: I don't think you can.

Colin is silent, he gathers his things and goes to leave.

LISA: Colin!

COLIN: David.

LISA: What?

COLIN: My name's David actually. What is it?

PAUSE

LISA: Nothing.

He leaves. Lisa lies on the bed looking at the ceiling.

SCENE 16

THE FLAT.

John is watching a video. Lisa has just returned from her meeting with Colin.

JOHN: You're going to be late to open up. Where were you?

LISA: Colin.

JOHN: I thought he'd cancelled this afternoon.

LISA: He changed his mind at the last minute.

JOHN: And you ran over.

LISA: Just as well I did. He's not coming again. He's emigrating.

JOHN: You sound upset.

LISA: No.

JOHN: Will you replace him?

LISA: I don't think so. I don't need the money. Why? Do you want to find someone else for me?

JOHN: What?

LISA: I thought Colin was your idea.

JOHN: Why do you say that?

LISA: Just a guess.

JOHN: Well, you know I'm not the jealous type.

LISA: You prefer it don't you?

JOHN: Maybe but I didn't think you'd fall in love.

LISA: I didn't.

JOHN: What's he do?

LISA: I don't know.

JOHN: He never told you anything?

LISA: Nothing.

JOHN: After all this time? I didn't think he'd stay.

LISA: Why not?

JOHN: He asked for someone young, 'childlike' were his words. You've changed, you're not at all 'child-like' now.

LISA: No. What about you? I'm surprised you've not left
             me for someone younger.

JOHN: So am I.

LISA: Suzanne.

JOHN: The new girl? What about her?

LISA: Nothing. I've just watched you watching her.

JOHN: So? She's very pretty.

LISA: So are the other girls.

JOHN: She looks sweet.

LISA: Sweet and innocent.

JOHN: Only she's not. She reminds me of you at that age.
             A little flirt. Pretending not to understand. It drives
             men crazy.

LISA: Maybe I didn't understand. Maybe Stella didn't
             understand either.

JOHN: Stella? Who's Stella? Oh that. You didn't really believe that did you? I thought you'd forgotten that.

LISA: Sorry?

JOHN: Is that why you turned down my proposal? Oh Lisa! You silly girl! I thought you said no because you didn't want to be tied down, with kids. You can see how I thought that. You're a very independent woman. I thought I'd hate it at first, but I like it. I like it a lot. I like what you've done to me.

LISA: I haven't done anything to you.

JOHN: But about that kid.

LISA: Stella. Her name was Stella.

JOHN: I'm terrible with names. Do you really think I'd hurt a kid?

LISA: Sorry?

JOHN: I know it's hard to understand but I didn't kill her. I might have felt like doing it. I might have fantasised about having her and she was a cheeky little madam. But I had nothing to do with her death. You don't have to believe me.

LISA: Why did you tell me you did?

JOHN: I suppose it was part of the fantasy. To have someone believe it. I don't know. I don't understand why I feel these things.

Don't look at me like that. I haven't done anything. Fantasy is one thing. I didn't actually do anything.

You believed it? Then you've used it to get exactly what you want haven't you?

You've got half, more than half the business. There's other money stashed away. The accountant told me, he worked for me before he worked for you. I let you do it. So what?

Did you think I was frightened of the police? They'd never have had me for it. I was in the club that evening. You never even bothered to check. I knew you'd never shop me. You didn't have the guts. It was easier to despise me and milk me for every penny I've got.

(mocking her) 'Maybe I didn't understand.'

LISA: I was sixteen. I was a child. I believed you wanted to look after me. Instead you used me as part of your sick fantasy.

You've destroyed whatever innocence I had. Every

bit of trust.

Everything is gone...

JOHN: Look, if you really thought I'd done it why didn't you go to the police years ago? You were happy to live with me. Happy to live with a man who you believed murdered a thirteen year old kid. What does that say about you eh? What does that say about you?

Lisa picks up a knife from the table.

LISA: I do this out of love for you. Do you understand?

She thrusts it into his stomach.

              It feels better this way doesn't it? If it hurts a little?

She lets go of the knife; he falls back, surprised.
She sits down and looks at the blood on her hands.

LISA: And fear them not which kill the body, but are not able to kill the soul: but rather fear him which is able to destroy both soul and body in hell.

SCENE 17

JOHN'S FLAT 1989.

Martin and Lisa are in Martin's bedroom.
Lisa is still wearing a coat and has a half-empty rucksack next to
her.

MARTIN: Maybe you should ask your dad to take you back.
Until you find somewhere else.

LISA: You don't understand. He won't talk to me. He
can't bear to look at me, or touch me.
Just being in the same room made him crazy. He
said he felt sick.

MARTIN: Have you tried asking anyone else?

LISA: There's my auntie but she won't help. She's too
scared of dad.

MARTIN: What about your friend Nikki?

LISA: I've been to Nikki's - she had this big row with her
parents. I could hear it all. They were saying her
father can't have thrown her out without good
reason - it's not our responsibility.
I left.

MARTIN: Have you spoken to any of the teachers about it?

LISA: They'd only tell social services - there's nothing they can do, I'm over sixteen now.
Will your dad blow up if he finds me here? Will he take it out on you? I don't want to get you into trouble.

MARTIN: No. It's not that. What are you going to do for money?

LISA: I don't know.

MARTIN: You can't sign on.

LISA: I'll have to get a job. I'll start looking next week. You're worried about your dad aren't you?

MARTIN: No.

LISA: What then?

MARTIN: I just think you should be with family, with people who care about you.

LISA: Like you.

MARTIN: Lisa!

LISA: It's true. No-one else wanted to come to the clinic
                with me.
                If you hadn't come I'd have been stuck in that
                bloody awful room on my own. They thought you
                were the father didn't they?

MARTIN: So what ? Is there really nowhere else you can go?

LISA: Martin! I've just told you.

She gets up and picks up her bag, she's near to tears.

MARTIN: I'm sorry.

Martin puts his arm around her.

LISA: Everything still hurts so much. The names he called
                me.
                The way he talked you'd've thought I'd killed
                someone. He thinks I did.
                He made out it was as though I'd slept with
                everyone in my class instead of one boy just once.
                He didn't believe me. It hurts when he won't see
                me, who I am. Do you understand? He sees this
                awful thing, this monster. But I'm still me. He was
                shouting about some tart and I didn't know who he

was talking about and then I realised it was me, he meant me!

He thinks before I was good and after I was bad....

MARTIN: Don't take any notice. You're just Lisa. O.K?

LISA: He kept saying I was only a child..

MARTIN: He wants you to stay a child because when you grow up you'll see him for what he is.

LISA: It's something else too. Something about me being his little girl. His perfect little girl.

Now he can't even touch me, look at me.

Please let me stay Martin.

MARTIN: It's O.K. It's not that I don't want you to. I just thought you'd be better off with a girl friend, or family. Not me and dad.

LISA: Does he know about you?

MARTIN: I don't think so.

LISA: Do you think he'd throw you out if he knew?

MARTIN: I don't know. Probably.

LISA: We could get a flat together.

MARTIN: And pay the rent with what?

LISA: Are you going to get a job?

MARTIN: I've got an interview tomorrow, cosmetics factory.

LISA: I thought you'd get somewhere better than that.

MARTIN: It's only for the summer. If I can earn enough in August I might go to Italy in September, on a dig. Did I tell you? That's what I've decided I'm going to do? Underwater archaeology. There's tons of stuff under the Med just waiting to be discovered. I need to save up for subaqua lessons too.

LISA: You can't swim can you?

MARTIN: I'd have to learn at the same time. I'm talking like this and I haven't had the results yet.

LISA: You'll pass. What time does your dad come home?

MARTIN: Depends how busy they are. Sometimes not at all.

LISA: He runs a pub doesn't he?

MARTIN: Not quite. It's a club, a sort of night-club.

LISA: I've never been to a night-club.

MARTIN: Never?

LISA: Dad wouldn't let me. I only went to the fifth form party because he went to see the headmaster and made him promise there's be no drink or drugs there.

Have you been to this club?

MARTIN: No.

LISA: Why not?

MARTIN: Not my thing. It's more of a champagne bar.

LISA: I like champagne.

MARTIN: You can get tired of it.

LISA: So you think it'll be alright with your dad.

MARTIN: Yeah. If I have to put up with the girls he brings back, he can cope with one friend of mine.

LISA: He brings back girls!

MARTIN: Sometimes.

LISA: My dad thinks sex is evil.

MARTIN: That's his religion.

LISA: He thinks I'm evil because I've had sex.

MARTIN: That's just stupid.

LISA: It's always the girl's fault. If someone we knew got pregnant he'd say, 'boys cannot control themselves - it's up to the girls to say no'

MARTIN: And what if they won't take no for an answer?'

LISA: You have to have 'moral authority'. 'A jewel of gold in a swine's snout, so is a fair woman which is without discretion.' That's what he ended up shouting at me.

They laugh

MARTIN: Come here and cwtch.

Lisa climbs into bed with Martin and cuddles up.

LISA: Will your dad think I'm your girlfriend?

MARTIN: I don't know.

LISA: Shall we pretend I am?

MARTIN: Don't think so.

LISA: Yeah, that's a stupid idea.

There's the sound of a door opening and closing.

LISA: What's that?

MARTIN: It's dad.

He puts out the light.

LISA: What did you do that for? I'll have to meet him sooner or later.

MARTIN: There's plenty of time. Go to sleep.

LISA: But -

MARTIN: SLEEP!

LISA: If you say so. Night night.
Lights fade. Silhouette of John is visible. Slow blackout.
The End

GIANT STEPS

Othniel Smith

Dedicated to the memory of Raymond Smith

Giant Steps was premiered by Made In Wales at Oval House, London in November 1998 before going on to play Chapter in Cardiff, with the following cast:

ALAN - Peter Savizon
OLIVER - Farimang Singhateh
GITA - Aileen Gonsalves

Director - Jeff Teare
Designer - Carolyn Willitts
Lighting design - Crin Cranston
Company Manager - Rebecca Gould
Stage Manager - Jo Nield

Giant Steps won a London Arts Board Diverse Acts Award.

CHARACTERS:

OLIVER MUNONYE -   A public-school educated West African, 27

ALAN McKENZIE   A Black Northerner, 27

DR GITA MUKHERJI   Welsh-born Asian, 32

Scenes One and Four are set in a private hospice.

Scene Two is set in a minor private school.

Scene Three is set in a police station holding-cell.

Scene 1 takes place a the present time.

Scene 2 takes place around ten years before Scene 1.

Scene 3 takes place around five years before Scene 1.

Scene 4 takes place a few weeks after Scene 1.

All the music comes from John Coltranes "Giant Steps".

ACT ONE

John Coltrane's "Naima" starts to play. Somewhere in the middle, Alan, wearing an expensive-looking sweatshirt and jogging-trousers, wearing tinted spectacles and carrying a walking-stick, comes on into a light.

ALAN: So I walked into his room. And he wasn't there. Which I already knew, because they'd told me when I came in the front door. But I wanted to see for myself. Just in case. Or maybe I've just got too used to walking into empty rooms. I've done a lot of that in my life. Well, either that, or walking into rooms full of people who really wouldn't mind seeing me dead. Which is much more fun. It's amazing what you can get used to, when you have to. So, anyway, I walked into his room. As I'd been doing virtually every day for about... six weeks. Since I got here and discovered him. Re-discovered him. And he wasn't there. Typical - I'd missed the whole thing. Story of my life. And his absence was... almost tangible. Like a bad smell. No. Like... like the lonely darkness at three o'clock on a December morning. Yes. That's better. A touch more poetic. I think that's the only thing we had in common - both our lives were like... bad poetry.

139

SCENE ONE

He turns and looks as a hospital bed is revealed. Oliver lies in it,
obviously very ill and very tired. He is attached to a drip-feeder. He
has a weak smile on his face as he listens and responds to the music. He
has a remote-control device which is controlling the CD-player. As the
piece ends, Oliver raises the remote-control - Alan rushes and grabs it
away from him.

ALAN: Now, now. Too much of a good thing!

OLIVER: ... "Too much of a good thing?" A ridiculous
                   notion. An entirely fictional concept, dear boy.
                   Invented by the puritanical and hypocritical in order
                   to control the masses.

ALAN: Seven times you played that tune. Now - I love the
                   great man as much as you do, but there is a limit.

OLIVER: I lost count.

ALAN: I know you lost count. You're doing a lot of that
                   these days.

OLIVER: Am I? Oh. I apologise.

ALAN: I don't want you to apologise, Ollie. Just... just get

140

a grip, that's all. Just don't... lose it.

OLIVER: I lost it longer ago than I care to remember, dear heart.

ALAN: None of that, either.

OLIVER: Oh, she's so sensitive.

ALAN: I'm warning you.

OLIVER: I'm so frightened. Mummy, please, don't let the horrible big man hurt me.

ALAN: I'll pull your plug. Then you'll be sorry.

OLIVER: But not for long.

ALAN: Ho ho. Just... just get a grip, alright?

OLIVER: I've got as much of a grip as I need, thanks all the same. If I want to listen to a tune seven times in a row, I will. Seventy-seven times, if I so desire. Seven hundred and seventy-seven times. Seven thousand, seven-

ALAN: Alright, alright, I get the picture. Just... just have a little consideration for the neighbours, alright?

OLIVER: If you find it so offensive, ask to be moved to a different room. This isn't a prison, you do pay their salaries.

ALAN: I don't want another room. I like my room. I've got it just the way I want it. If I moved somewhere else... well, I'd have to take all my dirty pictures down, I'd have to fiddle with my TV aerial, I'd have to get to know new people... I can't be bothered with all that. Life's too short. Ho ho.

OLIVER: What is it about the British, and their infuriating habit of stating the obvious at every possible opportunity?

ALAN: Don't knock it, man, it's our culture. Go and live in Russia, if you don't like it.

OLIVER: I didn't say I didn't like it. I said it was infuriating.

ALAN: Anyway - if I moved, I couldn't pop in and see you as often as I do. I know how much you look forward to my little visits.

OLIVER: Oh yes. I ache when you're not here. Mind you, I ache when you're here as well. Let's face it, I just ache, generally.

ALAN: Kids today. Whinge, whinge, whinge. *(pause)* The post's been. That Miles Davis I ordered has arrived. Pretty good, I gave it a couple of plays.

OLIVER: I didn't hear anything.

ALAN: No, well, some of us believe in earphones, you know? Some of us have a little common courtesy. *(pause)* Did you, er... did you get any letters?

OLIVER: Letters? I never get letters.

ALAN: Yes, I know, but... I thought you just might... you know. I thought you might have heard from... your family.

OLIVER: My what?? Please, no, don't say anything to make me laugh, it would probably kill me.

ALAN: I was just wondering.

OLIVER: Look - she won't come over again.

ALAN: I don't know what you're talking about, mate. (<u>pause</u>) You're pretty sure about that, then?

OLIVER: Absolutely.

ALAN: Oh. I was just... concerned about you. It's about time you had another visitor.

OLIVER: When's the last time *you* had a visitor?

ALAN: Ah, but it's different for me, see. I'm street-scum, me. I'm a loner, a rebel. I've spent my whole life storming the gates of oblivion, man. You don't have time to make friends when you're storming the gates of oblivion. It's a full-time job.

OLIVER: Still. I'm glad to see you made it.

ALAN: ... Ho ho. No news, then?

OLIVER: My family don't need to send me news. They're paying my way here. They are fulfilling their obligations. I'm duly grateful.

ALAN: She's not coming over again, then?

OLIVER: My baby sister is engaged to be married to a barrister.

ALAN: Barristers aren't so hot. I could reel off the names of half a dozen crap barristers I've come into contact with. Of course, some of them may have been crap on purpose, but I've never been one to hold a grudge. *(pause)* I could write to her.

OLIVER: Look - why are you so interested? You spoke to her for... what, ten minutes?

ALAN: She's pretty.

OLIVER: I watched you as you talked with her. You didn't spend a lot of time looking at her face.

ALAN: What can I say? Your kid sister has enormous breasts. I've always been a sucker for breasts. Ho ho. Damn fine behind on her as well. A real woman, you know? Not like these skinny bints you see in the magazines. A man wants something to hold onto, you know, a man needs warmth, a man needs... cushionage. If you know what I mean. Oh, sorry, I forgot who I was talking to for a second.

OLIVER: No need to apologise. You were only insulting the only woman I've ever loved.

ALAN: I wasn't insulting her. I was... I mean... she's obviously very intelligent, as well. And... well, she's very concerned about your welfare. That's why I thought... you know.

OLIVER: My father will have forbidden her to make further contact.

ALAN: Yeah, but... she's a big girl. Grown woman, I mean.

OLIVER: A grown woman who can't afford to be disinherited.

ALAN: Family life is a wonderful thing. Just goes to show. My folks had nothing, your folks are dead rich. My folks didn't believe in anything, your folks are big Jesus types. My folks were beaten down by racial prejudice, your folks live in a totally unmixed area of Black Africa. My folks are bastards, your folks are bastards. It's a funny old world, and no mistake.

OLIVER: My family... no. Forget it.

ALAN: Damned handsome woman, your sister. Did you ever fancy her?

OLIVER: Is there no end to your depravity?

ALAN: Never had the chance to find out, mate. No, I was just wondering. I fancied mine for a while. She's three years older than me. So, just at the moment at which I was becoming aware of the secondary sexual characteristics of myself and others... there she was! Poing! Wandering about the house in her bra and pants, leaving the door half-open when she had a bath... is it any wonder that I took to wandering the streets in search of other things to occupy my mind?

OLIVER: So, it's all her fault, eh?

ALAN: Not at all. I take full responsibility for myself. Anyway, she got pregnant, and everything started to... grow in the wrong directions. She lost her bounce. That's what it is about women, you know. The bounce.

OLIVER: "The Bounce - All You Ever Wanted To Know About Women But Were Too Stupid To Ask", by Professor Alan McKenzie.

ALAN: It's true, though. They're always so... dainty about everything. The way they walk. That wiggle - now, nobody has to wiggle. I don't wiggle - even you don't wiggle. Why should they?

OLIVER: How do you know I don't wiggle?

ALAN: Trust me. You don't.

OLIVER: When did you last see me on my feet?

ALAN: You're not a wiggler, Ollie. I can tell. Now, your sister... well, it's less of a wiggle than... a sway. A regal sway. A magnificent sight to behold. Some women keep it, you see. They stay wiggly, they retain their bounce. Girls like my sister, though... it's the curse of the proletarian classes. Child-birth leading to brain-death, and the loss of interest in anything beyond either the geographical or intellectual reach of the video and the refrigerator. The more I think about it, the more I'm glad I never had kids. You know, glad I was never responsible for doing that to a woman.

OLIVER: The world also breathes a sigh of relief.

ALAN: Of course, it happens to men, too. But women seem to admire that kind of thing in a man. Makes them feel safe. Unthreatened. Know what I mean? Of course you do.

OLIVER: Frankly, I'm proud of never having threatened a woman.

ALAN: Some of them like it, of course. I hate that. I mean, feminism is all well and good, but it's women who do women in. Men just stand by, with smug grins on their faces.

OLIVER: You've been watching daytime television again, haven't you? I've warned you about that.

ALAN: So what's the alternative? Read a good book?

OLIVER: A good book never hurt anyone.

ALAN: That's a joke, right? Ever heard of the Bible? The Koran? Mein Kampf? Jeffrey Archer?

OLIVER: I wasn't thinking. I'm... very tired.

ALAN: Anyway - I've been having to cut down on my reading. My eyes are starting to hurt. Nothing drastic, but... I'll leave you in peace, then, shall I?

OLIVER: No, there's no need for that. You... you amuse me.

ALAN: Awfully glad to be of service, your lordship. And while we're on the subject, you really don't pay me enough.

OLIVER: You're the one with the private income.

ALAN: No such thing. Savings, that's all. Savings.

OLIVER: I... I don't know why I talk to you.

ALAN: You've got no-one else to talk to, old son.

OLIVER: Ah yes. I knew there was something.

ALAN: ... Listen... I don't blame you, you know. For despising me.

OLIVER: I don't despise you, Alan.

ALAN: I mean, you've got every reason to.

OLIVER: Perhaps I have. But I don't have the strength to use them all at the same time.

ALAN: You do what you have to do in life, you know?

OLIVER: I know.

ALAN: You've got to survive. With... dignity.

OLIVER: And the other thing.

ALAN: What other thing?

OLIVER: The thing that's the opposite of surviving. One has to do that with dignity as well.

ALAN: Exactly. Well, obviously. I mean, we're both here, aren't we? Lap of luxury. All mod cons. Hot and cold running nurses, all preferences catered for. I'm sure you have to do a screen-test to get a job in this place. Everybody's so bloody beautiful. Even the cleaners look like they've just stepped off the cover of GQ. Or maybe they just pay them properly. In a hospital, too. The whole world's gone crazy.

OLIVER: What on earth is the matter with you, lately? You sound as though you've swallowed a party political broadcast.

ALAN: I've been thinking, that's all. I mean, you must have heard me, I'm only next door. Ho ho. I mean... I was always a thinker. But... something like this... your priorities change. I've been... thinking about God.

OLIVER: Yes. Of course. You're bound to, the situation being as it is. Fortunately, I spent the first eighteen years of my life thinking about God, and all the conclusions I reached are stored in my head, for ease of reference at appropriate moments.

ALAN: I don't think we're supposed to come to conclusions, Ollie. The questing spirit of humankind, and all that. We're supposed to keep on asking questions, up until the very last breath.

OLIVER: Asking questions is too much like hard work. That's why we employ men in dresses to do our thinking for us.

ALAN: I suppose *you* must have thought of becoming a man of the cloth. You know, when you realised. About yourself.

OLIVER: The wide choice of exotic headgear, you mean? Ready access to impressionable boys?

ALAN: I wasn't talking about that, Oliver, give me some credit. I meant... you know. Withdrawing from the world. From... temptation.

OLIVER: I did think about entering the church. But that would have been dishonest. Not that I have any objections to dishonesty, it's just that I've never been very good at it. Anyway, there were more attractive options. When I looked at what my London friends were doing :- publishing, music, the theatre, advertising...

ALAN: That's it, see. Public school. You build up useful contacts. Not that I didn't, in the institutions I attended. Where to go to get a gun. Who's the most reliable pimp. Who imports the best quality porno videos.

OLIVER: Oh, I had one of those contacts. I think he turned out to be the most useful of the lot.

ALAN: But it all comes back to the fact that it isn't a level playing-field. So, you go with the flow, you follow the path of least resistance, you take the road more travelled.

OLIVER: I thought you assumed full responsibility for yourself.

ALAN: I'm not blaming society. Society acts in order to protect itself, to cover its arse.

OLIVER: Ah. And you are a threat to the arse of society. That's something else we have in common.

ALAN: Why do I get the feeling you aren't taking me seriously?

OLIVER: Darling, I take you very seriously.

ALAN: Don't call me that. I'm not your fucking darling.

OLIVER: It's a figure of speech. You're really not my type.

ALAN: Yes, I know your type. Weedy, pimply white guys
            with thick-lensed glasses and washed-out hair.

OLIVER: What? Oh, you mean Rhys? The one who came to
            visit me? Oh, he's just a friend. One of the gang.
            And... well, he wasn't always weedy. He didn't
            always have bad skin.

ALAN: Oh. I'm sorry.

OLIVER: He's gone to live with his parents. He's going to
            last a lot longer than they think. He just wants to
            make them feel guilty.

ALAN: Ah. I like him better already. *(pause)* So, what is
            your type, then?

OLIVER: Oh, really. Are you truly so shallow?

ALAN: I've told you my type. A big woman. That's what I
            like. Do you like big men? Or would that be...
            awkward? You know, like on those videos.
            (American accent) "Oh my goodness - it's so big!"

OLIVER: I refuse to take further part in this conversation.

ALAN: Or maybe you don't see people that way. Maybe

you respond to individuals rather than types. That must be good. Being in constant contact with the class of person who sees you as an individual. And not as a type. I've had a spot of trouble in that area, over the years. It's profoundly frustrating.

Gita enters, in a white coat, a stethoscope around her neck, carrying a clipboard.

GITA: Morning, peasants.

ALAN: Hey, right on cue!

GITA: I'm sorry, Mr McKenzie?

ALAN: I was just talking about frustration.

GITA: My personal life is no concern of yours.

ALAN: I was talking about myself, Doc. I know almost nothing about your personal life. Not that I wouldn't want to.

GITA: How are you feeling today, Oliver?

OLIVER: As well as can be expected, Doctor.

ALAN: How come you call him by his first name?

GITA: You should think yourself lucky that I talk to you at all.

ALAN: I do, I do.

GITA: Has he been making a nuisance of himself, Oliver?

OLIVER: He's most entertaining. Like a good supermarket claret. He makes up in value for money for what he lacks in taste and quality.

ALAN: Have I just been insulted?

GITA: I sincerely hope so. (*She goes to check Oliver's drip, etc.*) Are you sure he's not bothering you? Because if he is, there are steps we can take to make sure he stops.

ALAN: More of them experimental drugs, eh, Doc? Mind you, that's how I got here in the first place.

OLIVER: He doesn't bother me. Really. Deep down, you know, he's an absolute sweetie.

ALAN: It's true, it's true. I'm just... misunderstood.

GITA: You do spend a lot of time in here. People will start to talk.

ALAN: Yeah, I just can't keep away. We should have one of them death-bed weddings, you know. Dead romantic. Ho ho.

GITA: It wouldn't be the first time.

ALAN: ... What, here? That spooky old chaplain? I had him down as a "Hell and Damnation" merchant.

GITA: Not him. Somebody from the local Humanist Society comes and says a few words. It's rather moving, actually.

ALAN: "Rather moving, actually." Slightly patronising, what?

GITA: And you're the very last person in the world to whom I'd come for a lecture on ethics, Mr McKenzie.

ALAN: Ah, well, then you'd be very unwise. I've seen life from both sides, you see. As a criminal, and as a victim; as one who has taken advantage of the misfortunes of others, and as one who is, himself, deep in shit. Perspective. That's the key.

GITA: Has he been boring you with the meaning of life again?

OLIVER: He hasn't quite got round to that, yet.

ALAN: Give me time, though, eh? Still. If only you could.

GITA: I'm sorry?

ALAN: Time. If only you could give us time.

GITA: I'd give you thirty years hard labour.

ALAN: I'd serve it gladly. As long as you were one of the screws. Ho ho. Have you ever been inside a prison? I think everybody ought to give it a go. Especially all these people who whinge on about how cushy it is. Especially those who get paid to send people there.

GITA: And what difference would that make?

ALAN: Well, none, probably. But that wouldn't be the point. The point would be... you see, if there's one thing I hate, it's people who go on and on, and don't know what the fuck they're talking about.

GITA: Pretty big on self-hatred, are you?

ALAN: The difference between me and them... is that I don't condemn.

GITA: You've probably condemned dozens, if not hundreds of people to death by selling heroin and crack to them, Mr McKenzie.

ALAN: I don't see you picketing any cigarette factories, Doctor Mukherji. I don't see you planting bombs underneath Mr Kipling's Range Rover. Lung cancer and heart disease kill many times more people than heroin and crack do.

GITA: I'm not getting into this argument.

ALAN: It isn't an argument. I was saying something outrageous for effect. Outrageous, but still true. What's also true is that I am a complete shit. Right?

GITA: Absolutely.

ALAN: How long did you work in the National Health Service, Doctor Gita Mukherji, B.Sc., M.D., University of Wales College of Medicine?

GITA: What's that got to do with anything?

ALAN: And how long have you been working in the private sector? You don't have to tell me. Longer, right? Right?

GITA: Yes.

ALAN: A lot longer?

GITA: Comparatively speaking. I'm not as old as I look.

ALAN: And what class of person can afford the kind of lavish, long-term medical care that you and your colleagues provide so altruistically? Rich people, right?

GITA: Not necessarily.

ALAN: But primarily. No-one's here at the expense of the state, are they?

OLIVER: You're fighting a losing battle, Doctor.

ALAN: You spend your life serving rich people. And how do people get to be rich? By being shits, right? Or by being related to a shit. Tell me I'm wrong.

GITA: You disgust me.

ALAN: That's a pity. Because I fancy you something rotten.

GITA: *(To Oliver)* Bedbath in half an hour, alright?

OLIVER: I can hardly wait.

ALAN: How come I never get bedbaths?

GITA: Your time will come, Mr McKenzie.

ALAN: ... Ooh. You cow.

GITA: *(To Oliver)* And Doctor Morgan will be round to see you later.

ALAN: Morgan? Now, there's a man with style. Those suits. That Porsche. He's younger than you, isn't he? Odd, the way he seems to have a far greater disposable income. I don't suppose his intimate relationship with a certain pharmaceutical company would have any bearing on that?

OLIVER: More drug trials, Doctor?

GITA: Well, that's up to you, Oliver. Don't let him blackmail you into anything.

ALAN: "After all, you're already half-dead, mun, what possible damage could it do?" He's a man for fuck's sake, he's not a fucking albino rat.

OLIVER: How dare you! I am noble and self-sacrificing, bestowing life upon others even as I drift towards the inevitable.

ALAN: Oh, of course. The old "God's brownie points" gambit. Clever.

GITA: Isn't it odd, Oliver, how Mr McKenzie has picked *this* particular phase of his life to develop a puritanical attitude towards drugs?

ALAN: My attitude towards drugs has always been a realistic one. Just because a drug is legal, that doesn't make it good; just because a drug is illegal, that doesn't make it bad. I'm quite happy with my medication as it is, thank-you very much. Anyway, you don't want a miracle cure, do you? It'd fuck up all your statistics.

OLIVER: He's only teasing, Doctor. Ignore him.

GITA: Excellent advice. (*she prepares to leave*) About Doctor Morgan... well, it's up to you, Oliver. I'll see you later.

She starts to leave. Alan stands in her way.

ALAN: Do you know something, Gita? Nobody ever wanted to have sex with me until I had money.

She pushes past him, and exits.

ALAN: She wants me.

OLIVER: Obviously.

ALAN: Honest, she's gagging for it.

OLIVER: Well, I suppose you'd know about that kind of thing.

ALAN: She's not married, you know. Not married at thirty-two. Just the right age for me - just those few years older, just enough miles on the clock. Hasn't got a boyfriend either, I asked around. And she's not a lesbian.

OLIVER: How can you tell? Because she wiggles? Lesbians wiggle, I've seen them.

ALAN: I asked around. It's tragic. Handsome woman like that going to waste. Just because her vast intelligence intimidates men. Plus she probably earns more than most Asian guys in her social bracket. Not good for the old male ego. Wouldn't bother me, though. Yes, she'd be perfect if only she wasn't Welsh.

OLIVER: I thought you only liked big women.

ALAN: I didn't say I *only* liked big women. I like big women. I also like little women. And medium-sized women. Size isn't everything, you know. I like... brainy women. That's why your sister's perfect for me. Big and brainy.

OLIVER: Was that true? What you said. About... your sexual history.

ALAN: ... Yes, it was true. I mean, look at me. I'm not exactly Mr Universe, am I? *(pause)* No, no, you see, what happens is, I say "I'm not exactly Mr Universe", and you leap in and... oh, please yourself.

OLIVER: I cannot tell a lie. You are not exactly Mr Universe.

ALAN: I see. It's at times like these that you find out who your friends are. (<u>pause</u>) So you wouldn't have fancied me, then?

OLIVER: Please don't speak in the past tense. It's very insensitive.

ALAN: Sorry. But... you know. In your... cruising days.

OLIVER: Cruising? I never went cruising. I met people, I made friends with them, if we liked one another in that way, we slept together. And there weren't that many... are you asking me if I find you attractive?

ALAN: Not at all. I was just wondering... if you would have found me attractive, had I been into that kind of thing. Which I'm not. Not that there's anything wrong with it. But I'm not. I hope I've made myself quite plain?

OLIVER: No. God made you quite plain.

ALAN: Ho ho.

OLIVER: Aren't you always telling me that women never liked you? So why should men like you?

ALAN: Makes sense. Still, logic and sex seldom go together do they?

OLIVER: You see, Alan... in many ways... in many ways, you're an appalling person.

ALAN: Stating the obvious, Ollie? It's rubbing off on you.
              It's just... this place, though. All these pale, skeletal
              young men with wealthy parents... the way they
              look at me... it's all about class, isn't it?

OLIVER: Class? Obviously not, since you're here.

ALAN: Thank-you, but that's not what I'm talking about. I
              mean... how come you and me are the only Black
              guys in the whole place?

OLIVER: Just lucky, I suppose.

ALAN: I mean - if you were the evil drug-dealer, and I was
              the inoffensive homosexual, neither of us would be
              here, right? I'd be rotting away in a shitty bedsit
              somewhere, and you'd have had sense, you'd have
              had connections, you'd have been able to launder
              your assets and get into art or property. Before you
              got dragged down the pit.

OLIVER: I was born gay, Alan. You weren't born an arsehole.

ALAN: Ah, but... I've been thinking you see. About what
              did make me what I am. About... options. And
              priorities. And possibilities. And injustices. And...
              guilt. And... why I don't feel any guilt. Self-pity,

yes, but that's not exactly a recent development. See, in the old days, when I used to think, it always used to lead me in the same direction. But now... I can see all the different paths I could have taken. And I think about what would have happened if I had taken them. And I think... I'd still have hurt people. Because that's what life is, either you do the hurting, or you get nailed. And I never made a very good victim. (*He looks at Oliver, whose eyes are closed.*) Are you asleep?

OLIVER: Yes I am. Piss off.

ALAN: Very well. Let it not be said that I can't take a hint. Enjoy your bedbath. Still, I suppose you'll have that big German bloke, so you're bound to. Pervert!

OLIVER: Criminal!

ALAN: And keep that bloody music down!

As Alan leaves, Oliver uses his remote control to turn the music on again - Coltrane's "Countdown", very loudly. Alan turns and glares at Oliver, who is smiling. Alan exits.

Gita enters and signals for the music to stop

GITA: The music wasn't that loud, not really. Sound-proofing, you see. Alongside cable television, extensive menus to suit all tastes, tender loving care from our dedicated team of hand-picked professionals... the almost complete absence of cockroaches. It's a good place. I'm doing some good. Making people feel better. Plus, I'm getting a bit of research done, as well. The possible side-effects of combining psycho-pharmacological medication, anti-depressants, say, and medication designed to treat, or rather, to control physiological symptoms. I've been promised publication in an American journal if I can get my graphs right. Oh, and the money's not bad here, either. No, I tell a lie. The money's bloody brilliant. There, I've said it. I mean, it's not excessive, it's just about... fifty percent more than I need. Which is ideal. And the work... well, it's certainly stressful. Puts you through the emotional wringer. But you get time to breathe. To smell the roses. To learn to like people. Yes, to be brutally frank, you get a nicer class of patient in a place like this. Perhaps it's something to do with the voluntary element. People have chosen to come here. And rich, dying people are less inclined to violence than the clientele in my last job. I can still picture the moment:- I was off guard for a second, having just saved a man from choking to death on his beer-flavoured vomit, when, with a mercifully clumsy movement, he attempted to slice off my left breast with a cunningly-concealed Stanley knife. It was at this point that I decided to leave the NHS. I mean, it wasn't much worse than any other Saturday night in casualty, but I figured - why bother? There are easier ways of getting your karma sorted. People here seem less inclined to racial abuse as well. Or maybe they're just more polite. Which is all I ask of anyone I'm not looking to play Naked Twister with. Oliver wasn't especially different from the other tragic, middle-class gay boys in my care. Less silly and shallow than a lot of them, but silliness and shallowness can be very charming. Obviously, otherwise they wouldn't have landed up here. I liked Oliver, though. I liked him a lot. Even though he was obviously past his best by the time I got to know him. But then, so was I. He did tell me that he and Alan were old friends, after a fashion, but I thought it was just him being delirious. He did a lot of that towards the end. But no. "Eshu!", he said. "Gesundheit!", I said, as he'd expected. Then he explained. Eshu is an ancient African deity. Almost but not quite a Yoruba version of Satan. His job is to go out into the world, and keep tabs on people. To examine their lives, and make them pay for their arrogance, their fecklessness, their dishonesty. Not that Oliver was

into all that pre-Christian stuff, obviously. But he
did wonder how it was that Alan always seemed to
turn up at pivotal points in his life. And I said,
"Perhaps it's you turning up at pivotal points in
his." And he looked at up me, and he said, "Oops!"

She leaves.

SCENE TWO

*A small, disused classroom is revealed. Two desk, a couple of chairs.
Alan comes in, very angry, followed by Oliver, who is subdued. Both
are wearing dirty football strips, each has a different-coloured shirt.*

ALAN: Bastards!! Bastards, bastards, bastards! (*he kicks over
              a chair*) Fucking... fucking bastards!! (*he picks up a
              chair, whirls it around his head, and hurls it into a
              corner*) BASTARDS!! (*he walks around, still worked
              up. He sees the other chair, makes as if to pick it up.
              Immediately, Oliver sits in it. Furious, breathing
              deeply, Alan glares at Oliver.*) And what the fuck do
              you think you're doing?!

OLIVER: I am sitting down.

ALAN: Get up!

OLIVER: No.

ALAN: GET UP!!

OLIVER: I want to sit down. We're going to be waiting for quite a long time. I would like, at least, to be comfortable in the interim.

ALAN: ... You... you're fucking unreal, man.

OLIVER: Very probably.

Alan glares at him for a while, then moves away. He goes to look out of the window.

ALAN: This is fucking brilliant, this is. Can't even see the game from here. Fucking brilliant.

OLIVER: It's rather a foregone conclusion, is it not?

ALAN: What are you on about?

OLIVER: You always beat us.

ALAN: Hey - don't bag me up with the rest of those losers.

OLIVER: You would rather appear to have bagged yourself up with them.

ALAN: Yeah, well, not for long. Two more months, that's all. Then I'm never going back. I'm not like them.

OLIVER: I'm pleased to hear it. Anyway, according to the records, with respect to this particular fixture, it is my team which would appear to be the losers.

ALAN: I think you're confusing me with someone who gives a shit.

OLIVER: Every game, so far. In nineteen years. Except for the last one. Which was a nil-nil draw. We had a rugby tour cancelled, so there was a little more defensive muscle available than usual.

ALAN: Ooh. Swish. Rugby. Wugger. Oh, Woderick, Wichard, Waymond, do come and play wugger with me!

OLIVER: Yes. Highly amusing. Of course, ours is only a scratch team. Made up of those unwilling or unable to go home for the holidays. So I suppose, in a way, we're rather in the same boat as you lot.

ALAN: Snotty little bastard, aren't you?

OLIVER: I am neither snotty, nor little, nor a bastard.

ALAN: Still. At least you're going to get what I'm going to get. Worse, probably. I mean, I suppose they expect better behaviour from you. Me, I'm just another faceless savage. Which is fine by me.

OLIVER: Of course.

ALAN: Meaning what?

OLIVER: Nothing.

Alan approaches Oliver, assuming a threatening posture.

ALAN: I'm warning you, mate. I'm fucking warning you. There's no-one watching us now, there's no-one to fucking come between us now!

OLIVER: I do wish you'd moderate your language. Profanity for its own sake is both tedious and counter-productive.

ALAN: You... you think you're fucking clever, don't you?

OLIVER: I'm... moderately intelligent. Honestly. Britain must the only country in the world where to refer to someone as "clever" is on a par with calling their mother a whore. No wonder they lost the Empire.

No wonder they get splinters in their fingers, scratching their heads over what went wrong.

ALAN: You're... you're foreign!

OLIVER: Thank God.

ALAN: I didn't know you were foreign. I wouldn't have given you such a hard time if I knew you were foreign. Where are you from?

OLIVER: Isn't it obvious? Iceland.

ALAN: Seriously.

OLIVER: I was born in Iceland. My father used to be a diplomat.

ALAN: ... Diplomat, eh? Fucking different world. Diplomat.

OLIVER: Do you know what a diplomat is?

ALAN: Yes, I know what a fucking diplomat is. A diplomat is... somebody who's got a diploma.

OLIVER: I do hope that was a joke.

ALAN: Civil servant, isn't it. Sent over to foreign countries
to lick arses. There's not a lot I don't know about
the big, wide world. Nothing but Graham Greene
in our library. Stupid buggers that run the place,
they think just because a book is old it won't have
any sex or violence in it. I swear some of those
bastards wouldn't know one end of a book from...
the other end. So, where are you really from then?
Is your dad dead rich, then?

OLIVER: He's very rich, yes. Fat, and rich, and ignorant and
brutish.

ALAN: Just like mine. Apart from the rich bit, obviously.
You're African, then, are you? What's it like in
Africa? Don't tell me - just like Britain, only not so
many Black people. Ho ho. No, really. What's it
like?

OLIVER: I'll send you a list of useful books on the subject.
Assuming that you really can read, of course.

ALAN: Oh, I can read, alright, matey. And I can write, too.
What if I was to write my name in your blood all
across that wall?

OLIVER: We'd both be in even more trouble than we are already. This is your stock-in-trade, is it? Mindless violence? Because, frankly, you don't do it particularly well.

ALAN: I'm not a criminal. I'm a scholar. I like books. Unfortunately, in my deprived social position, I've no choice but to steal them.

OLIVER: Ah. And the concept of the public lending library has not yet reached the British Isles? We've had them for years in Africa.

ALAN: Libraries are slow. Takes months to get new stuff in. If you want to keep on top of things, there's no choice but to be a grubby, thieving bastard. Sad fact of life. Listen, mate... I... I wouldn't have kicked you all over the pitch if I'd known you were African.

OLIVER: Ah. Is that what's known as positive discrimination?

ALAN: I thought you were... you know. Some rich kid.

OLIVER: I am some rich kid.

ALAN: Yeah, but you're some African rich kid, not some bourgeois, capitalist sell-out, class traitor bastard, shit-soft Southern English rich kid.

OLIVER: And this is somehow worse than being a privileged African?

ALAN: Obviously. In this country, you have to betray people to get rich. Unless you're rich already, of course. Which is a whole other kind of scumbag. It's all about class, you see.

OLIVER: Ah yes. Your class system. Most amusing. The hours of amusement I've given my schoolmates by eating my soup with the wrong fork. And as for betraying people... my father became rich through manufacturing and marketing skin-lightening creams. For Africans who don't want to look too African. That is what is paying for my education.

ALAN: Whoa. Heavy shit. Still, that's capitalism for you. Or the will of Allah.

OLIVER: My father is a Christian.

ALAN: Ah well. Now you're starting to make sense. Mind you... (*rubbing his jaw*)... you've got a good left hook on you for a Jesus freak.

OLIVER: I'm rather proud of it, I must admit.

ALAN: Listen... I'm sorry about... you know. Hassling you. On the pitch. I was out to get you, plain and simple.

OLIVER: I did notice.

ALAN: I was checking you out, you know. Checking out how tough you were. I mean, I didn't know if you were any good or not. Our coach hasn't been doing his job. I mean, he's supposed to do research, isn't he? The danger men up front, the potential holes in the defence, current league form. Fucking hopeless. Bastard useless alcoholic failure.

OLIVER: He sounds rather like our coach. Although he probably earns rather more than yours does, so I expect he can afford to be a better class of alcoholic, at least.

ALAN: Is he your headmaster?

OLIVER: Please. Our headmaster? Association football? Far too plebeian.

ALAN: The team seem pretty keen, though. Crap, but keen.

OLIVER: Oh, well. Those of us who play football tend to be the lower class of public schoolboy. Nouveau riche. The sons of pop musicians and road haulage magnates.

ALAN: I see. Anyone famous?

OLIVER: I wouldn't know. I have not the slightest interest in road haulage.

ALAN: You know what I mean.

OLIVER: I know nothing about pop music. I like jazz.

ALAN: Jazz?!! Now, what the fuck is jazz all about?!

OLIVER: Does it have to be about anything?

ALAN: It has to be about something more than sharp suits and fancy fingerwork, man. Jazz... it's supposed to be the cry of the downtrodden, man, the defiant voice of the ghetto, kicking ass, demanding respect. From what I can gather these days, it's a lot of middle-class Norwegian bastards with PhD's in musicology.

OLIVER: You seem to know an awful lot about absolutely everything.

ALAN: I told you. Books. Anybody can open a book...

OLIVER: (*holding out a hand*) I think it's time we formally introduced ourselves. Oliver Munonye.

ALAN: (*taking and shaking the proffered hand*) Alan McKenzie. Pleased to meet you. Sorry about... you know. Earlier.

OLIVER: Not at all. I shouldn't have hit you.

ALAN: No, well, I shouldn't have tripped you.

OLIVER: And I shouldn't have provoked you by playing so brilliantly.

ALAN: And I shouldn't have knocked you over that time you had a clear shot at goal.

OLIVER: Oh, you were only doing your job.

ALAN: I was doing it too well. I mean... this was just a skive, you know. Break in the routine, bit of fresh air. The very last thing I wanted to do was actually win the game for the bastards. But once I saw you, man, I just had to get in there.

OLIVER: Yes, this event isn't really about sport, is it? It's about... rich kids showing the poor kids what you get by "playing the game", poor kids kicking the stuffing out of the rich kids, and everybody going home happy, having done their bit for a classless society. Well, none of us actually goes *home*, but you know what I mean. A rather shoddy, poorly managed piece of public relations for two outmoded institutions. A good day out.

ALAN: You're a bit of a leftie, aren't you?

OLIVER: I'm sure it's just a phase. I'm at that difficult age, you know.

ALAN: I wonder if there's such a thing as not being at a difficult age? I'd like to know, just for future reference, like.

OLIVER: I expect not. Life is hell, and then you die.

ALAN: I bet you're a brilliant laugh in the dorm at night.

OLIVER: Oh yes. Non-stop squealing in the dorm at night.

ALAN: I can believe that. The things I've heard about public schools. Mind you, it's not that different at my place.

OLIVER: What's not that different?

ALAN: You know. Lads. Suddenly discovering what all their bits are for. And only having each other to try them out on.

OLIVER: It can't only have been books.

ALAN: You what?

OLIVER: The reason you've been... detained.

ALAN: The reason I'm "detained" is that I got caught.

OLIVER: But there must have been more to it than books. They wouldn't have had you incarcerated for stealing books, surely. They'd have given you a medal.

ALAN: Well... I didn't just steal books for me. Once I found out how easy it was. Students, you see. Students need books. Students have no money. I made myself useful to them, I provided a service. I've sacrificed myself on the altar of higher education. *(pause)* Oh yeah, then there was the heroin, as well.

OLIVER: ... Drugs?!

ALAN: It just happened to be lying about the place. Well, I say lying about. Stashed inside a hollowed-out Harold Robbins. Worst mistake of my life. If it had actually been a good book, the pigs would have ignored it, see. "Ooh, Harold Robbins. I see you're a man of taste, McKenzie. Oops - what have we here?" Of course, I'd actually bought that one. Irony, huh?

OLIVER: You're a drug-addict?

ALAN: Nah. Not heroin. Horrible stuff. Only tried it twice. Smoking it, you know? First time, I was sick. Second time I was even more sick. Can't see the attraction. Only morons get hooked on that shit.

OLIVER: But... other drugs?

ALAN: Oh cut the "innocent" crap, African. You go to a public school, man, they're famous for it.

OLIVER: They're famous for a lot of things I've yet to come into contact with. A liberal education, for one thing. I've never seen any evidence of drug-taking. The very thought scares me stiff. I've never even drunk alcohol.

ALAN: Yeah, well, you've had it easy, haven't you? I mean,
               when you live at shit-level, sometimes you've just
               got to get out of your head, you know? It's a cliché,
               but that doesn't mean it's not true. Drugs or telly,
               bingo or religion - sometimes you've just got to get
               out of your head.

OLIVER: So, how long are you in for, in total?

ALAN: Six months, repeat offender. Mind you, it was the
               first time they caught me with drugs. They take that
               kind of thing pretty seriously but it was obvious I
               wasn't supplying... Your face! You're actually
               scarted!

OLIVER: Of course I'm scared. I've spent all afternoon
               indulging in physical combat with a gangster!

ALAN: I'm not a gangster. You need a gang to be a
               gangster. I don't have the social skills required to be
               a gangster. Plus, I'm not a hard man, no matter
               how much I try and pretend. And I'm not stupid
               enough to trust people. (*Wandering around, he idly
               opens the desk.*) See, the more untrustworthy you
               are, the more you have to depend on people. I can't
               be doing with.... bloody hell!

He takes out a small, lacy brassiere, and holds it up, in amazement.

OLIVER: Ah, now, I think I can help you with this item. It's a weapon - a slingshot. You know, like the story of David and Goliath in the Bible. Except, with that, you can throw two stones at once. Fiendishly clever.

ALAN: This is a girls' school! This is a fucking girls' school!! A private fucking girls' school. Oh, man, this is like a porno movie come to life.

OLIVER: Erm, I hate to deflate your, ahem, mood; however, I have to remind you that it is half-term. Consequently - no girls.

ALAN: Well, you never know. There might be some spare ones ligging about. You know, Mummy and Daddy too busy entertaining Lord and Lady Fartington-Smythe to have them cluttering up the house. Or maybe the odd Arab princess, who's missed her plane. Hey, do you suppose they wear suspender-belts, under those great big chador things? That's what I like about the veil. You can use your imagination. I mean, don't get me wrong, I'm all for the short skirt, the tight sweater, the figure-hugging denim trouser. But... it's like... the difference between listening to a pop song on the radio, and sitting and watching the video. Sometimes... sometimes, it's just more fun to use

your imagination, do you know what I mean? I'm
rambling, aren't I? Sorry. My mind starts wandering
when I think about girls.

OLIVER: Yes. So does mine.

ALAN: Have you got a girlfriend? I have. Well, I did. Sort
of. Well, we talked a lot, anyway. I used to go in her
Dad's shop. Naima, that was her name. I mean, we
never actually went out or anything. We might
have, though. Eventually. When she was old
enough. I was even looking into converting to
Islam. Just on the off-chance. But her Dad sent her
off to Pakistan to get married to some geriatric
goat-herder on the fucking North-West Frontier.
Really pissed me off, that did. Still. Plenty more fish
in the sea.

OLIVER: There's a jazz tune called "Naima". By John
Coltrane.

ALAN: Yeah? Any good?

OLIVER: Exquisite.

ALAN: I'll have to look out for it, then. In the meantime,
however... *(concealing the bra in the sleeve of his
shirt)*... I'll have to make do with this. Oh yes. This

will be very useful, to be going on with.

OLIVER: Useful? Oh! Ugh! You're disgusting!

ALAN: It's a fact of life, Ollie. For every human being, and most species of mammal. Sometimes, you just have to get down with your bad self, man.

OLIVER: Ugh! You're... nauseating.

ALAN: I may well be. But at least I'm at ease with myself about it.

OLIVER: Meaning?

ALAN: You know what I mean. Mr Public Schoolboy. Hey, maybe they're watching the game from some secret vantage point somewhere.

OLIVER: Watching our game? Who could possibly be so starved for stimulation?

ALAN: Teenage girls are every bit as weird as teenage boys, man. Stands to reason. Hey, maybe... *(He goes to the door, looks out and around)* That's strange. *(He goes to the window.)* But... but... the bastards!

OLIVER: I'm sorry?

ALAN:　　　The bastards! Shit! I hate that.

OLIVER:　　What do you hate?

ALAN:　　　Oooh. That's terrible. That makes me so mad.

OLIVER:　　What does?

ALAN:　　　Answer me this question, Ollie - where are we?

OLIVER:　　In a rather dingy little room.

ALAN:　　　Yes, but where? Geographically?

OLIVER:　　I would presume that we're at some point vaguely equidistant between my school and your detention centre.

ALAN:　　　Detention centre. Hold that thought, Oliver. Why am I in a detention centre?

OLIVER:　　Because you're a victim of society?

ALAN:　　　Leaving that aspect of things aside for a second...

OLIVER:　　Because you're a criminal.

ALAN: Ding! Correct. Now... what happened out on the pitch?

OLIVER: We had a minor altercation, and were sent off.

ALAN: And where were we sent off to?

OLIVER: Well... here. A dingy little room.

ALAN: And who came with us?

OLIVER: That pineapple-complexioned warder of yours.

ALAN: And where is he now?

Oliver gets up, goes to the door.

OLIVER: He's gone.

ALAN: Exactly. Now - here I am, a convicted criminal stroke victim of society, in an unguarded room, in a deserted school, a girls' school at that, in the middle of nowhere. Here's the question - in my situation, what would any self-respecting juvenile delinquent do?

OLIVER: Well... escape?

ALAN: Exactly! Any self-respecting juvenile delinquent would try and escape.

OLIVER: Oh. Right. All the best, then.

ALAN: Ah - but that's just it, you see! That's what they want me to do! They want me to try and escape! They want me running around in the wilds of... the frigging Welsh Borders, or wherever the fuck we are! They want to catch me, tattered and shagged out, in two days time! They want to rough me up a little as they help me into the police-van! They want to drag me into court and increase my sentence by another year! This is... this is... persecution!!

OLIVER: Or perhaps they trust you.

ALAN: Yeah, right!

OLIVER: Perhaps they know you're intelligent enough to foresee the consequences of running away.

ALAN: Well... how dare they?! How dare they presume... I hate that. That makes me so fucking mad!

OLIVER: It makes you mad that people trust you and consider you intelligent?

ALAN: Those people, yes. Those smug, ignorant bastards. They've out-manoeuvred me. I hate that!

OLIVER: Well, look at it from my point of view. My school think so much of me that they've left me alone in a room with a violent convict. I'm deeply moved.

ALAN: ... Oh yes. Ho ho. I'd submit a formal complaint about that, if I were you. That's racism, that is. If you were some pasty-faced son of a High Court Judge, or a Tory M.P., they wouldn't have left you alone with me. Although, of course, someone like that might have leapt at the opportunity.

OLIVER: What do you mean?

ALAN: Oh, don't come the innocent, Ollie. I mean, look at me. Prime stud material, me. Solid rough trade, that's me.

OLIVER: I'm sorry, I don't understand.

ALAN: Oh, don't be obtuse, man. Public schoolboy. You know what I'm talking about.

OLIVER: I'm afraid I don't.

ALAN: Oh, I was forgetting. They don't have

homosexuality in Africa, do they? Your women are so beaten down that you can slip it to them any way you like, and you won't hear a word of complaint.

OLIVER: You really do know absolutely everything, don't you?

ALAN: Pretty much.

OLIVER: You don't know anything! You don't know anything at all!!

ALAN: Alright, alright, calm down.

OLIVER: You don't know anything!

ALAN: Okay, okay, man. I admit it. There are a few gaps in my knowledge. Quantum mechanics remains a closed book to me. I'm not that clued-up when it comes to spot-welding. And, despite constant research, I'm still unclear about the precise difference between metaphysics and epistemology.

OLIVER: You... you don't know anything.

ALAN: Look... look... are you having... you know... problems, or anything? I mean... do you want to talk about it? It's not like I can help or anything, you know, my personal life isn't exactly... hey... do you want to know a secret? I've never had sex. *(pause)* Well, you could try and look surprised. I... I mean, I could have. Round our way there are girls who'll do it for the price of a bottle of cider. Kids, I mean, not proper women with proper tits or anything. I was saving myself for Naima, though. I'm sure we'd have got round to it.

OLIVER: I've done sex. Sex is over-rated.

ALAN: Really? Well, you know what they say. If you think sex is a pain in the bum, you must be doing it wrong. Ho ho. Hey, back home, was it? With a big, fat African woman? I'm going to get myself sorted with someone like that when I get out. I know just the man to organise it for me. Bit of a sick bastard, but they have their uses. Naima was chunky. I like that. They're all big in my family. My mum, my sister... I took a polaroid once, of my sister getting out of the bath. Tried to sell it... but, it's like the Mona Lisa you know? People would love to buy it but there's just not that sort of money around. Still got it actually. Laminated it, to protect it from natural wear and tear.

OLIVER: You are an appalling person. I'm... I'm glad I hit you. When I did it, I wasn't sure you deserved it.

Now, I know you did, so I feel better about it.

ALAN: Alright, alright, calm down, man. No need to be so uncivil.

OLIVER: You... you... I was feeling sorry for you as well, you know?

ALAN: I can manage without your pity, mate.

OLIVER: I was making allowances for you, your deprived background, the half-hearted education system in this country, your obviously limited intelligence...

ALAN: Now, now. No need to be snide. And we were getting along so well.

OLIVER: I'm not interested in getting along well with you.

ALAN: What's the matter? Don't you fancy me? *(Oliver aims a punch at Alan, and misses; he aims another one, which also misses - Alan grabs his fist.)* Violence is not the answer, my friend. Look - it's not a crime not to like women, you know? Most men don't like women. It's just we've all got different ways of dealing with it. The way you lot do it is just another option, that's all.

With his free hand, Oliver punches Alan in the stomach. Winded, Alan falls to his knees. Oliver goes and sits in the chair, head in hands. Recovering slowly, Alan looks at him, and is ignored. Alan gets to his feet.

ALAN: And I thought I had problems. I really ought to... no. Why waste my energy. Fuck it, I'm not staying here. I'm going for a wander around. I'm going looking for... (*he shouts the next word in Oliver's ear*)... Girls! Maybe catch the end of the game. You.. you want to get yourself fucking sorted out, mate.

He exits, still in pain. Oliver continues to sit, deep in depression. He starts to cry.

Music - "Naima" by John Coltrane.

ACT TWO

SCENE THREE

Music - "Mr P.C." by John Coltrane.
A time vaguely equidistant between Scene 1 and Scene 2. Alan and
Oliver are in a police cell. Both are wearing suits, but no ties or shoes.
Alan sits in a corner of the cell, in dark glasses, apparently tranquil.
Oliver is pacing the floor, in a state of agitation.

OLIVER: This is... this is intolerable. This is absolutely... this
is scandalous. I will not stand for this. This is... it's
too much, it really is. They can't do this to me. Not
to me. This is... this is... oppressive. (*He stops, looks
at Alan*) Look, is that all you're going to do? Sit
there? (*No answer.*) This is an infringement of my
human rights. I thought this was supposed to be a
civilised country! They're always criticising us for
being undemocratic. Hypocrites! That's all they are,
hypocrites! (*Alan chuckles to himself.*) And what's so
amusing? (*No answer*) They'll rue the day they ever
tangled with me. My family is not without
influence. I am not without influence. The things I
could say in open court, the names I could name...
they'll be sorry they ever screwed around with me.

ALAN: Names?

OLIVER: I'm sorry?

ALAN: You said you could name names.

OLIVER: Oh, you can't imagine.

ALAN: Can't I?

OLIVER: You cannot possibly imagine what names I could name.

ALAN: Like who?

OLIVER: What?

ALAN: Give me an example. Of a name.

OLIVER: I can't do that. They're not going to get me that way. I'll say it in open court, not before. They're not going to fool me, with their... spies.

ALAN: ... Spies?

OLIVER: That's what I said.

ALAN: You think I'm a police spy? Me? Do I look like a police spy?

OLIVER: If you looked like one, surely that would defeat the object. Although, of course, there's always the double-bluff. And the triple-bluff.

ALAN: I think you spend too much time in front of the telly.

OLIVER: I am not as stupid as I may look. They'll learn that to their eternal cost.

ALAN: Have you forgotten? We were both arrested at the same time.

OLIVER: Of course we were. Entrapment. That's what it was. It's a well-known technique. To entice someone into committing a crime, then arrest them. It happens all the time. It's happened to a number of my friends.

ALAN: In public toilets, eh?

OLIVER: ... Yes. In public toilets. There. Are you satisfied? Some of my friends are homosexual. I am homosexual. Is that what you want? Are you pleased with yourself?

ALAN: I've often wondered about that. These cute coppers in public toilets. When do they actually make the arrest? Before, during, or after? "You are not obliged to say anything, as I can see that your mouth is full."

OLIVER: I suppose you find this very amusing.

ALAN: Not really. Tiresome. Boring. Nothing to laugh at at all.

OLIVER: Someone's going to pay for this. When my lawyer arrives. Someone will pay.

ALAN: Daddy.

OLIVER: I beg your pardon?

ALAN: Daddy's going to pay.

OLIVER: Oh, you don't know what you're talking about.

ALAN: I'm afraid I do. I've seen it all before. A tale as old as time itself. Changeless as pondwater, tarnished as tuppence.

OLIVER: You've been arrested before, then.

ALAN: I'm a police spy, aren't I? It's my job to be arrested. I've never done the public toilets thing, though.

Not pretty enough.

OLIVER: Oh, you're not a spy. You're just a grubby little drug-dealer.

ALAN: Grubby, is it? Obviously, this grubbiness hadn't yet manifested itself when you attempted to buy cocaine off me.

OLIVER: *(looking around, alarmed)* SSSSHHH! Don't say things like that. There'll be video cameras, microphones.

ALAN: You attempted to buy cocaine off me.

OLIVER: Will you be quiet?!

ALAN: No crime was committed. The body searches will have confirmed that for them. Of course, I expect you enjoyed yours.

OLIVER: ... Meaning?

ALAN: Meaning you're obviously more used than I am to having your most intimate regions probed by eager male fingers. It was an unsubtle heterosexist jibe, my friend. I'm sure you're not unused to that kind of thing.

OLIVER: Are you trying to tell me you've never been searched before?

ALAN: Not for a long time. Nowadays I employ people to undergo body-searches on my behalf. Much more satisfactory.

OLIVER: Damn! I'm so angry. This was all completely avoidable.

ALAN: Well, yes. If you hadn't tried to buy drugs off me...

OLIVER: Well, if you'd... if you'd got a bloody move on about it, there wouldn't have been a problem.

ALAN: It was my night off. I was out, enjoying myself. I don't get out much. I was trying to have a good time. I was trying to find myself a woman. People hassling you for illicit substances all evening. It gets on your nerves.

OLIVER: I was told that you were the man to go to.

ALAN: I may or may not be the man to go to. But not on my night off. And I wouldn't have sold you anything anyway.

OLIVER: And why not?

ALAN: You're a brother, man.

OLIVER: You're no brother of mine.

ALAN: I know what's in the stuff, man. Honestly. The number of people I've seen convinced they can fly, with half an ounce of industrial bleach up their nostrils. One laughs until one cries.

OLIVER: Oh, I see. So you're not a drug-peddler at all. You're just a swindler. Well, that's alright then. That's wonderful. We can all go home, no harm done.

ALAN: You aren't a druggie, Oliver.

OLIVER: ... How do you know my name?

ALAN: Trust me. I know a druggie when I see one.

OLIVER: How do you know my name!?

ALAN: You are Oliver Munonye - I claim my crisp five-pound note. I know everything about you, Ollie. I'm a spy, aren't I, I live in your wardrobe. You really must do something about that dry rot.

Oliver goes to Alan, grabs him by the lapels.

OLIVER: How... do you know... my name?

ALAN: I saw it, I saw it. When they made you turn out your wallet. On your precious-metal-coloured credit card. Right next to your impressive ready-to-wear rainbow selection of condoms. "A good scout is always prepared. Dib dib dib, dob dob dob." (*Alan chuckles. Oliver lets go, and moves away*). I wasn't going to sell you any drugs, Ollie.

OLIVER: ... Why is it so bloody cold in here?

ALAN: It's a cell. If the pigs made it too inviting, they'd never get rid of people. They'd be queuing up to get arrested. Contrary to suspicion, that's not really what they want.

OLIVER: We have fundamental human rights. Don't we?

ALAN: We're criminals, man. We have forfeited our rights.

OLIVER: We haven't been charged with anything. They can't keep us here.

ALAN: Can't they? Don't tempt them... Look, don't worry man, they're not going to charge us.

OLIVER: You can read their minds can you?

ALAN: Yup, I've got my microscope right here... I've had experience of how they do things. You see, they wanted to arrest me for dealing drugs. But I wasn't dealing drugs when they apprehended me - there weren't any drugs on my person, they won't find any in my car. They'd even now be tearing my flat apart if they knew where it was.

OLIVER: There's always the small matter of assault.

ALAN: Well, look at the facts:- two skinny black men, approached by three large white guys in jeans and big boots? How did we know they were police? They didn't identify themselves until we were halfway through kicking their ass. Procedure, you see. They fucked up. So, they'll keep us here, to learn us a lesson, and then, when our lawyers arrive, they'll let us go. End of situation.

OLIVER: ... How can you be so calm about everything?

ALAN: I know I have nothing to fear. *(pause)* Hey - you hit that ginger one a good left, though. Have you been practising?

OLIVER: I know how to take care of myself. My father
                taught me. He was a boxer, in his army days.

ALAN: Army, eh? Nothing like a chequered past. In thirty
                years time, they'll be calling this a chequered past.
                Rather than a criminal record and a bad reputation.
                How long was he in the army, your father? Is there
                compulsory National Service in your country? Was
                he in a civil war? They're always having civil wars in
                Africa, aren't they?

OLIVER: They're always having civil wars everywhere. (*He
                looks at his wrist - his watch isn't there*) Damn! What
                is the point of that? What is the point in taking my
                watch away? How am I going to kill myself with a
                watch?

ALAN: Many ways. You might have secreted a tiny cyanide
                capsule in the back of it, for just such an eventuality
                as this. You could sharpen one of the edges on the
                stone floor, and open an artery. You could smash it,
                and swallow the innards, and jump up and down,
                thus lacerating your internal organs. I mean, it's
                pointless, really. We're both wearing clothes, we
                could strangle one another with our trouser-legs.
                We could bash our brains out against the wall. We
                could call the duty sergeant, and tell him that his

wife chases army trucks. Sometimes... sometimes, I think that there are more ways to die than there are to live.

OLIVER: You know something? I wish you were as... enigmatic as you think you are?

ALAN: Enigmatic? There's no mystery to me, Ollie. I'm just a lonely man, making his entrepreneurial way in a corrupt society.

OLIVER: So that's how you justify dealing in drugs, eh? You are simply exploiting the corruption of others.

ALAN: I'm not justifying anything. I don't need to. Any more than you need to justify trying to buy drugs.

OLIVER: That was... that was... a mistake.

ALAN: Which was what I was trying to tell you when we were so discourteously interrupted.

OLIVER: I was... I was with friends. They're having a party, and they wanted... entertainment. We were told that you were the man to go to. Look... if you'd just sold me the stuff, we wouldn't be in this mess!

ALAN: I wasn't going to sell you any drugs, Oliver. Plain and simple. I have principles, you see. *(pause)* I don't know why I said that. It's not true. I tell myself I'm better than the scum who hang around playgrounds and council estates with carrier-bags full of crack. I tell myself I'm striking a blow for emancipation by concentrating on the places where well-off white people go. I tell myself I'm being ironic when I put on a good suit, and a big hat, and slip my gold tooth in. I'm not of course. I'm conforming to stereotype. We stampede for the safety of stereotypes, don't we? And... well... some of the scum of playground and council estate fame are... not unknown to me.

OLIVER: I was already aware that you were are an appalling person. Now I realise that, worse still, you are also pretentious.

ALAN: Your harsh words sting me, brother.

OLIVER: I've told you, don't call me that.

ALAN: Whatever you say, Ollie. *(pause)* Hey - do you want to see a rude photograph of my sister?

OLIVER: No, I don't.

ALAN: Have you got any sisters? Just wondering. *(pause.*

He starts to scat-sing, idly, Coltrane's "Mr P.C.".
Eventually, Oliver recognises the tune.)

OLIVER: Stop that.

ALAN: What's the matter? Not a Coltrane fan?

OLIVER: Yes, I am. Which is why I would like you to stop.

ALAN: Everyone's a critic. I bought a saxophone, you know. Soprano. Brand new. Bought the case, cleaning-cloth, polish, a book of solos. Got it home... couldn't get a note out of the thing. Well, a few fart noises. But you can't build a career on that. Contrary to what cynics might suggest. I persevered, though. After a month, I could get through "Old MacDonald Had A Farm", with virtually no mistakes. Sort of lost interest in the practical side of things, after that. Still, I now possess the shiniest soprano saxophone in Christendom.

OLIVER: I am deeply moved.

ALAN: You know your trouble, Ollie? You're self-obsessed.

OLIVER: Why shouldn't I be? I'm the most interesting person I know. Oh, where the hell is that bloody woman?

ALAN: Your lawyer?

OLIVER: She should have been here hours ago.

ALAN: It's a Friday night stroke Saturday morning, man.
           She's probably out getting laid or getting funky.
           Lawyers are human, too, you know. A little too
           human, most of the ones I know.

OLIVER: All she has to do is make a few phone-calls. It can't
           be that hard. I'm sure even you know how to make
           phone-calls.

ALAN: You've got a snide streak in you, Ollie. It's most
           unattractive.

OLIVER: I'm not interested in being attractive to the likes of
           you.

ALAN: This is the story of my life. I stand in the wilderness,
           and howl at the moon. (*he howls - a little too
           convincingly*) As Mr Neil Diamond so eloquently
           put it, "'I am', I said; to no-one there."

OLIVER: Neil Diamond?

ALAN: Hey, cut me some slack, man. I'm not at my best right now, okay?

OLIVER: Look - if you're unhappy, maybe you deserve to be, eh? Have you ever stopped to consider that?

ALAN: Well, you see, Ollie, here is where we encounter what is commonly known as the "chicken hyphen egg" scenario. Did my unhappiness turn me to evil, or is it my essential baseness which has led to unhappiness? We turn to our panel of experts - firstly, my father:- "You always were a worthless piece of trash"; secondly, the first police officer I ever had a conversation with :- "I've got my eye on you, you little black bastard!"; thirdly, the first woman I ever asked to go out with me :- *(he points, and laughs derisively)*. Does the prosecution wish to question any of my witnesses?

OLIVER: Self-pity always makes for a nauseating spectacle.

ALAN: You're a hard man to entertain, Ollie. I'll be forced to fall back on my stockpile of "queer" jokes, and I've always found that kind of thing so utterly distasteful.

OLIVER: You can't say anything to hurt me. Listen - after the things my father said to me, no-one can touch me.

ALAN: ... Yes. I understand that.

OLIVER: Oh, really. God save me from being understood by
                 someone as... no. I'm sorry.

ALAN: No, go on, say what you were going to say. I can
                 take it.

OLIVER: Please - I am being... I'm taking it out on you.
                 We're both here as a result of my stupidity.

ALAN: Well, you'll not catch me arguing with you on that
                 one.

OLIVER: I'm just... I'm so angry with myself.

ALAN: Will your friends be worrying about you?

OLIVER: Oh, they aren't really... they're just some people I
                 met. We were just going to...

ALAN: Blokes, were they?

OLIVER: They were all men, yes.

ALAN: You were going to have an orgy! Rampant gay sex,
                 and a cocktail of exotic drugs!! "I made my excuses

and left", writes our intrepid reporter.

OLIVER: We were going to have a party.

ALAN: Honestly. I'll say something for you bunch - you know how to have a laugh. Even in these bleak times.

OLIVER: I am not a "bunch". I am an individual.

ALAN: "I'm not a number - I'm a free man!" (*he chuckles. pause.*) Popular, are you?

OLIVER: I'm sorry?

ALAN: Popular. Do you have lots of friends?

OLIVER: Dozens.

ALAN: Oh. Good. Pleased to hear it. I've got friends. Some. They're all scumbags, though. Stab you in the face for a ten-quid fix. And the only women I've ever slept with have been prostitutes. Whether or not they realised it at the time.

OLIVER: Are you trying to make me feel sorry for you?

ALAN: You're judging me. I hate it when people judge me.

"Let him that is without sin cast the first stone."

OLIVER: I see. So, I'm a sinner, and you're a victim, is that it? Look, I realise that you're undergoing a crisis of conscience, right now, but I'm afraid you've picked the wrong time, the wrong place, and the wrong person if you want to talk through your personal problems. I have my own problems.

ALAN: Oh yeah? Like what?

OLIVER: Like none of your bloody business, that's what.

ALAN: Alright, I was only asking, only taking an interest in my fellow human beings. Only reaching out the hand of brotherhood... Oh I was forgetting. We're not brothers. *(pause)* So have you got a job Ollie?

OLIVER: I am training to be an accountant.

ALAN: Aaagh! Alright, alright, you win. I give up. Your problems are Mount Kilimanjaro compared to mine.

OLIVER: Was that supposed to be in some way humorous?

ALAN: I'm sorry, I'm sorry. I'm sure your family are very proud of you.

OLIVER: Yes. I'm sure they are.

ALAN: You must have encountered some very interesting people.

OLIVER: I'm sorry?

ALAN: All the names you're going to mention. In court. You must move in exalted circles.

OLIVER: Exalted? That isn't the word I'd use.

ALAN: Hey - we're both men of the world. We could both name names. We could both bring people down. Important people. People I've got drugs for. People whose secret sexual proclivities you're aware of. We should get together, man. We could bring down all the institutions...

OLIVER: You're being utterly ridiculous.

ALAN: Honestly, we could. I mean, the things I could tell you...

OLIVER: I'm not saying that I don't believe you. I'm saying that it's ridiculous to suggest that anything can be brought down that doesn't want to be. I mean, a judge resigns here, a politician there, things blow over. Well, I've seen it happen in my country. I've read of it happening in this country. People having accidents, just as they're preparing to blow the whistle. People falling under lorries. Accidents happen.

ALAN: ... And I thought I was paranoid! *(pause)* So, is that what you're going to do, then? Go back to Africa and get into politics?

OLIVER: Politics? Me. No. I did think about it once. But... I have made other choices.

ALAN: Ah. You... you met someone, did you?

OLIVER: I'm sorry?

ALAN: You met someone. Someone... special. Who made you feel good about... what you are. Sorry. Who you are. What happened? Did he break your heart?

OLIVER: He broke my heart, I broke his nose. It seemed like a fair deal.

ALAN: I thought I'd met someone. But... but it turned out I hadn't. And then it happened again. And it hurt even more. Still. We've all got our own shit to deal with, haven't we? And we deal with it in different ways. Oh, and by the way - I'm not a drug addict.

OLIVER: I never said you were.

ALAN: I mean, I'm a user. I... use. But not regularly. Just to cope with things. I mean... I'm okay. I mean... I'll be getting out of here in a couple of hours, I'll be alright then. No need to panic, or anything.

Oliver looks at Alan. He goes to him, takes off Alan's sunglasses. Alan does not look at him.

OLIVER: I... I do know you, don't I?

ALAN: Nobody knows me.

OLIVER: Look ... are you alright?

ALAN: I'm fine. Just ... just keep your mind occupied, that's the thing. Or if that doesn't work, try and empty it of everything. Can I have my glasses back, please. Can't see a thing with them on. *(Oliver gives him the glasses, which he puts on.)* Thanks.

OLIVER: Do you want me to call for somebody?

ALAN: No, no, I'm fine. I've managed before, I'll manage again.

OLIVER: But surely... aren't there medical obligations? Shouldn't the police... aren't there things which have to be done for you? I mean, if you're registered as a... you know.

ALAN: I'm not registered as anything. I don't even pay income tax. They can't track me down, see. I'm untrackable. To all intents and purposes, I don't exist. Well, on a couple of computers, maybe. But that's a different me. I'm a different me every day.

OLIVER: Look... do you need a doctor?

ALAN: Nobody needs doctors. Just think wholesome thoughts. Eat lots of roughage and oily fish. Is she nice?

OLIVER: What? Is who nice?

ALAN: Your lawyer. Describe her to me.

OLIVER: I don't... she's... youngish. White. South African. Went to Cambridge.

ALAN: Not that kind of stuff. What does she look like?

OLIVER: I... I don't... she looks like a vaguely attractive female.

ALAN: I think you're over-playing this gay thing, man.

OLIVER: I don't know what you mean.

ALAN: You're just being silly. I know a good-looking man when I see one. Doesn't mean I want to get down and dirty with him.

OLIVER: I don't look at people in that way.

ALAN: Really?

OLIVER: I really think you need a doctor.

ALAN: Is she blonde? I've never understood this thing about blondes. Hey - is it true that in Africa, at the sight of a golden-haired female, all men fall to their knees in worship?

OLIVER: Don't be absurd.

ALAN: Just checking. Has she got a good bum on her? You can't whack a good set of buns.

OLIVER: I don't care about her... all I care about is that she does her job, and gets me the hell out of this infernal place.

ALAN: Alright. Be like that. Just when we were getting pally.

OLIVER: Look... are you going to be alright?

ALAN: You mean am I going to go gaga? Am I going to run head-first into the ceiling? Am I going to rip your lungs out with my bare hands? Wish I had the strength.

OLIVER: I should shout for someone. They'll get a doctor.

ALAN: Oh, don't worry about me, Ollie. I'm fine. When my lawyer comes, he'll sort everything out. He's a good sorter-outer, my lawyer. When he's got his head together. Trouble is... he likes to enjoy himself. Bit of a party animal. Why, he's probably off his face in a gutter even as I speak. "I cite Dionysus as my noble precedent." Roman god of wine and unruly behaviour, you know. Or was he Greek?

OLIVER: Greek. The Roman equivalent was Bacchus.

ALAN: Aha! A classical education. You just can't keep it to yourselves, can you?

OLIVER: Look... when was the last time... are you... are you having withdrawal symptoms?

ALAN: Withdrawal symptoms? Only junkies have withdrawal symptoms. I'm just... trying to pass the time. Does she wear suits?

OLIVER: Does who wear suits?

ALAN: Your lawyer. I like the look of a woman in a suit. Does she wear tights? Don't like tights. Bare legs. Much nicer. Don't like these civil-engineering type bras either. And wigs. You'd be surprised how many women wear wigs. You're at the height of passion, reaching a crucial moment, all of a sudden, her hair-do comes off in your hand. That's the sort of thing that can give a man a complex.

OLIVER: I don't go out with women.

ALAN: Men wear wigs too. Old, vain men.

OLIVER: I don't sleep with old, vain men. Look... when they let us out... can we give you a lift? You're obviously in no condition to drive, or to walk the streets, come to that.

ALAN: That wouldn't be a good idea, Ollie. You'd be
           followed, you see. They want to find out where I
           live. I'm better off on my own. It's easier to lose
           them if I'm on my own. I'll have to dump my car as
           well, assuming they put it back together properly.
           Even if they don't plant drugs in there, they might
           stick a bug in it.

OLIVER: Talk about paranoia.

ALAN: It's not paranoia. I'm a bad person, Ollie. They're
           out to get me. With good reason. I've... I've done
           bad things.

OLIVER: So, if you feel so bad about it, why don't you stop?
           Why don't you give yourself up?

ALAN: I gave up on myself a long time ago.

OLIVER: That's not what I said.

ALAN: I know, I know. I was just being melodramatic. For
           effect. Truth is... I've already gone too far, made
           too many big deals, with too many big people. I'm
           in too deep, I'm trapped, I'm powerless to resist
           market forces. Everything's pushing me in one
           direction. There's only one way for me to go. The

only question is... how do I get there? Who decides? The only question is one of... control.

OLIVER: Erm... look... is there... is there can I do anything for you?

ALAN: You're not my type, Ollie. But thanks for caring enough to ask.

OLIVER: I meant... I was talking about...

ALAN: I know. I know what you were talking about. I'm sorry. I'm... just a little tired. Hey - do you want to know something?

OLIVER: Not especially.

ALAN: I'm not the worst person I know. I'm not even the tenth worst person I know. Can you believe that?

OLIVER: Yes. I can. Sad to say.

Alan chuckles, then rolls himself into a ball.

ALAN: If you leave before I wake up... give my regards to Iceland, eh?

He falls asleep. Oliver looks at him for a while, baffled. He takes off his jacket, covers Alan with it. He goes and sits on the other side of the room, his head in his hands. Music -"Naima" by John Coltrane, which fades as darkness falls.

Gita comes on.

GITA: I'm trying to think what I was doing five years ago. It's pretty hazy, actually. Pretty much the same as I was doing ten years ago - being 'my daughter, the doctor' - Trying to make my Mum proud of me. Which she is, I think... Although I still have this nagging suspiscion that she'd have preferred me to marry one... Trying to make my Dad notice me. I swear that since I got qualified he's down-graded all doctors in his mind. As though it can't be a big deal if I can manage it. As though there must be a trick to it... I remember, I was ten years old, and he brought out his big old chess set. "Here is a game that India has given to the world." Explaining about the pieces - the dispensable footsoldier pawn, the devious knight, the all-powerful queen. Except we'd done it all in school the year before, and I checkmated him within fifteen minutes, first game we played. "You've got the knack, very good." I was delighted - something we could do together. But, funnily enough, we never got round to that second game. He made a bigger fuss when my little brother passed his driving-test than he did when I

*she = JH7()
atrd)t 111@
Aan t
Oliver.*

got the results of my finals. Still - my mental
health's been a lot better since I stopped worrying
about that kind of thing. There comes a time in
everybody's life when you have to say to those who
would belittle you - "up yer arse". Pardon my
French. Not that he doesn't love me. I'm sure he
does. In his way. It's just... I get the feeling he's
frightened of the idea that I'm cleverer than him.
Not that I am, not really. He built up a good
business, you know, ethnic fabrics, that's not easy.
But... I should visit them more often, it's not far.
It's just... I used to find it irritating when they went
on at me for not giving them grandchildren - but
now my brother's provided them with three, I find
it irritating that they hardly bring the subject up at
all. They think I'm a lost cause. I think I agree with
them. Ten years ago, I was still hopeful. Despite
everything. A fresh-faced, bright-eyed medical
student. Combining optimism with spiritual
torment in that way that only the young can. Five
years later, I was still bright-eyed. But that was
mostly down to the amphetamines. Standard issue
for your much-dumped-upon junior hospital
doctor. Was I going out with anybody? Yes, when I
could find a ten-minute window in my schedule.
That would have been the anaesthetist, who used to
shout out "Bitch!" and "Whore!" and "Slut!" when
we were having sex. And the C word, which I swore

to my mother I'd never say out loud. No matter how much he begged me. This was before the one who wanted me to have a boob job, and after the one who could only achieve an erection if we were in a linen-cupboard. Something to do with the smell, I think. That warm, crisp, washing-powdery smell. I'm much better off out of it. Things are better now. A little house all to myself, a waterbed, a 29-inch television, a packed freezer compartment, a scenic bike-ride to work. And, on average, only two deaths a week. Which, I've discovered, is my limit, when it comes to allowing yourself to feel the pain, but not letting it destroy you. But other people's pain... well, that's always going to be a problem. Like when I walked into Oliver's room. And saw Alan there, staring at his bed. Pretending he hadn't noticed me.

SCENE FOUR

The private hospital room as in Scene 1 is revealed. Oliver's bed is empty. Alan stands, staring at it. Gita turns to him.

GITA: Mr McKenzie.

ALAN: (*not looking at her*) It's... it's raining out.

GITA: I know. I had to wear my water-proofs.

ALAN: Time of year. It rained a lot this time last year. I remember, I was... I was quite relieved. I was ill, you see. I was relieved that I didn't have to go out. I was glad that I had people to go out for me. By the time it got warm, I was better. Healthier. This time next year... well. One never knows, does one?

GITA: No. One never knows.

ALAN: I... I went to a football match on Saturday.

GITA: Really?

ALAN: I figured I might as well. Had to get out of the house, anyway. The looks I was getting. Never been to an actual professional game before. I used to ask my Dad to take me. When I was little. And he used to tell me to bugger off. He didn't do a lot of that over the weekend. Something to do with my bank-balance, I venture to suggest. Not a great match, it must be said. Nobody famous, or anything. The curse of the lower divisions, eh? And it didn't seem natural without the commentary. Still, it was good to feel... part of something. Even if it was something I wasn't greatly enthusiastic about. I don't expect I'll have the chance again.

GITA: I prefer rugby, myself. You're brought up on it
             here, whether you like it or not.

ALAN: Had a laugh on the train down.

GITA: Really?

ALAN: All these men in suits looking me up and down over
             the rims of their designer glasses. Wondering if
             there'd been some administrative error.

GITA: Travelling first-class, eh? I'll have to try it some day.

ALAN: You absolutely must. The seats are comfy enough.
             Mind you, the coffee still tastes like piss. Even if it is
             the lovingly cultivated piss of Tuscan virgins who've
             never drunk anything but the purest spring water,
             and never eaten anything other than that posh
             bread they make with olive oil. *(pause)* So... so
             when did it happen?

GITA: Saturday night. I... tried to get in touch with you.

ALAN: *(looking at her for the first time)* You can't have tried
             very hard.

GITA: I phoned the only number we had for you. It must

have been your sister that answered? She said she
didn't know where you were. Our priority was his
family.

ALAN: Saturday night. I was out. People-watching. No.
             Girl-watching. Drinking. Actually enjoyed myself.
             Did you... did you get his... he had a list. Of people.

GITA: He'd given it to me. Not a very long list. It didn't
             take long. You were the only one we couldn't
             contact. But then... well, we knew we were going to
             see you.

ALAN: Was it... did he... painful, was it painful?

GITA: We did our best for him.

ALAN: Your best? Your best to stop it from hurting? Or
             your best to keep him hanging on by a thread?

GITA: He did volunteer for those drug trials, you know.
             He wasn't doing it for his own benefit.

ALAN: You people. You can't just let someone... you've
             just got to squeeze that last bit of goodness out,
             haven't you?

GITA: Well, at least he had some goodness in him.

ALAN: I see. Alright, Gita. What if I tell you what you want to hear? I'm giving you advance notice, right? I want to be dead long before I'm dead. Do you hear me?

GITA: Absolutely.

ALAN: You keep that... that shit Morgan away from me. I don't want to catch the merest whiff of his cologne, do I make myself clear?

GITA: Abundantly.

ALAN: I'm serious.

GITA: I know you're serious. Don't worry. I'd be the very last person to...

ALAN: Unnecessarily prolong my life?

GITA: I... I'm sorry, I didn't mean to say that.

ALAN: You didn't. You haven't answered my question. Was he in a lot of pain?

GITA: No. No, he wasn't. Not right at the end.

ALAN: Good. I'm... I'm glad you were there for him.

GITA: Yes, well. Only doing my job.

ALAN: I suppose you must be used to it by now.

GITA: Yes. I suppose I must. Look, sit down, you must be shattered.

ALAN: I'll stand, if you don't mind. Stretch my legs a bit. Is he... Oliver's body...

GITA: They collected it last night. I expect he'll be home by now.

ALAN: Oh. So he's well and truly gone, then.

GITA: Well and truly. So. How was your weekend? All in all.

ALAN: Great. Apart from the family side of things. Which was hopeless. It's... it's almost as though they're just waiting... still. You aren't interested.

GITA: Alan... I'm your doctor. Things are going to get... we're going to have to learn to get on.

ALAN: I've never had any problems getting on with you,

Gita. I like you. I like you a lot. And I'm used to people I like not liking me. That's why... Ollie didn't judge me. He knew all about me, but... he liked me. I think.

GITA: I got into this game because I wanted to relieve suffering. And I look at you, who can only afford to be here because of the suffering of others... still. We've had this conversation a million times before.

ALAN: Have you got someone to love, Gita?

GITA: Not as such.

ALAN: What the fuck do you mean by that?

GITA: Cats. I have two cats.

ALAN: Ah. I see. You're a cat person. It all comes clear. Why did you come to work here?

GITA: Fewer hours, higher pay. In my old hospital... well, it was too hectic. I could feel myself losing touch with my humanity.

ALAN: Yes, well, there's humanity in shitloads around here.

GITA: You can say that again.

ALAN: Are you happy?

GITA: At the moment? Not so as you'd notice.

ALAN: Doesn't it suit you? Striking up relationships with gorgeous young men who aren't after your body, and who are going to die before they can start getting on your nerves?

GITA: Do you want the truth?

ALAN: ... No. No, I don't think so. I'm not sure I could handle the truth about you.

GITA: I don't know what the truth is. Except... when I go to bed, I find I can sleep. I look forward to coming to work. I've convinced myself that I'm doing some good. And that makes me feel...worthwhile.

ALAN: Complacent?

GITA: I know you think I'm a frigid bitch Alan, but I'm not that far gone, not yet.

ALAN: Are you a lesbian?

GITA: I don't think so. Still, there's plenty of time.

ALAN: Did you love Ollie?

GITA: ... Yes. I did. In my own way.

ALAN: Did he know you loved him?

GITA: You may have noticed, Alan, I'm not very good at concealing my emotions. Hardly ideal for someone who works... well, in a place like this.

ALAN: Did you cry? When he died?

GITA: I don't cry. I cried myself out years ago.

ALAN: Was it... was it horrible? When he died?

GITA: Not for him.

ALAN: Was someone holding his hand?

GITA: I was.

ALAN: Oh. Good. If... if I'd been here, would you have let me hold his hand? If he'd asked you to.

GITA: If that's what Oliver wanted.

ALAN: And how would you have felt about that?

GITA: My feelings aren't important. I'm not the one who's dying.

ALAN: I see. What if... what if I asked you to hold my hand? When my turn came? Would you do it?

GITA: Of course.

ALAN: Why?

GITA: Why not? It wouldn't cost me anything.

ALAN: You... you really hate me, don't you?

GITA: I hate what you exemplify. I've seen what drugs can do to people, Alan. To families, to communities. To... individuals. Friends.

ALAN: Yes, well, I've seen what years of poverty and neglect and enforced ignorance have done to families, communities, friends. But... no. You're not going to get me making excuses for myself, Gita.

GITA: Good. Your excuses are exceedingly lame, and exceedingly boring.

ALAN: Maybe I should try harder.

GITA: Maybe you should save your energy. Maybe you'll need it.

ALAN: Yes. Maybe. Who collected Oliver's body?

GITA: Somebody from his father's company. Not his sister, if that's what you were wondering.

ALAN: I liked his sister.

GITA: Yes. He told me. He said you liked her breasts.

ALAN: What I could see of them. She seemed like a good person as well. I don't meet many good people.

GITA: You do surprise me.

ALAN: You talked about me, then.

GITA: Talked about you?

ALAN: You and Oliver. You talked about me.

GITA: When there was nothing more interesting to talk about.

ALAN: What did he say about me?

GITA: He told me how much he lusted after your body.

ALAN: But seriously.

GITA: He told me... he felt sorry for you. I told him not to. I told him that you'd made your own choices. And he told me to consider what your life would have been like if you'd made other choices.

ALAN: What did you come up with?

GITA: Not a lot. He reminded me of something I already knew. That we aren't the only ones who make choices about our lives. And I reminded him... we're all in the gutter - but some of us are looking at the stars. And he laughed.

ALAN: ... I... I don't think I ever heard Ollie laugh.

GITA: No, well, you made him feel almost as uncomfortable as he made you feel.

ALAN: And there was me thinking it was sexual tension.

GITA: He was a serious young man. Twenty-seven years and two months of likeable, amusing seriousness.

There have been worse lives.

ALAN: I'll have to get you to write my epitaph as well.

GITA: How about:- "He was a bastard - and what's more, he was crap at it"?

ALAN: *(chuckling)* I wish... I wish I could be around to see you get married. To see what poor sucker you finally end up with.

GITA: Yes, well. I might not even be around to see that.

ALAN: You'll do alright. People like you always do.

GITA: People like me?

ALAN: People who already have everything. Look at you - beautiful, intelligent, well-off, conscientious, from a good, solid, middle-class family... you'll do alright.

GITA: We aren't middle-class. We're trade. There is a difference.

ALAN: Doesn't hurt, though, does it? Bit of money behind you. Bit of confidence. Posh accent.

GITA: Yes, well, that's more to do with the fact that my

mother scarcely ever let me out of the house till I went to primary school. Over-protective. I learnt to speak English from listening to Radio Four. And as for confidence... well, I'm glad I've succeeded in fooling you.

ALAN: Why would you want to fool me? I thought I was lower than the worms. Still. It won't be long before I get to discuss it with them in person.

GITA: Look... look, there's still time... you only have to say the word... the medication we have now... if you'd sought help at an earlier stage... people are living for -

ALAN: I was never very good at living. Why fight fate, eh? Don't you have any work to be getting on with?

Gita sighs and starts to leave.

GITA: I... when you go to your room, you'll find... Oliver said that you were to have all his compact discs. He never did quite succeed in explaining jazz to me. He gave me his books. The rest of his stuff... his clothes, his hi-fi... his father sent word that everything was to be incinerated.

ALAN: You aren't going to, are you?

GITA: Of course not. Oliver believed in the redistribution of wealth. There'll be some tramps walking around in very sharp suits.

ALAN: Yes. He'd have liked that. Gita... before you go...

GITA: Yes?

ALAN: Have you... have you ever slept with someone you were actually in love with?

GITA: Not since my first boyfriend. At university. He died. Someone sold him some bad drugs one night and he had a CVA. A cardiovascular accident. A stroke. He was twenty years old. He was planning to go into cancer research. He was... nice.

ALAN: I... I... I... didn't know about that.

GITA: Well, now you do.

ALAN: Oh. *(pause)* I'm sorry. Is that any use to you?

GITA: None whatsoever.

ALAN: Ah well. Worth a try.

GITA: I disagree. But, hey, thanks for caring.

ALAN: No, I... I do care. I mean... I know what it's like not having anyone.

Gita goes up to him, touches his face.

GITA: You know what you are, McKenzie? You're a fucking wreck.

She briefly kisses his lips.

ALAN: What did I do to deserve that?

GITA: Nothing to do with me. It was from Oliver. His dying wish. Well, one of them. (*she starts to leave*) Now, don't hang about in here. There's somebody else moving in this afternoon. They'll be frightened enough as it is without having to cope with your ugly mug, on top of everything else.

She exits. Alan sighs.

ALAN: A kiss. A patronising one, a pitying one, but still a kiss. Makes a change. From being kissed out of... avarice. (*he goes to the chair and sits, painfully*) Shouldn't sit down. Don't know if I'm strong enough to get up again. Anyway... (*he looks around* *the room*) ... look at it. Nothing left of you. Stripped clean, ready for the next poor bastard. Probably another pasty-faced posh bird. Another fucking Old English Queen. Looking at me like I'm from another planet. Which I might as well be.

He puts his head in his hands. Oliver enters, quietly, stands looking at him. He is wearing his family's tribal dress. Alan does not respond when he speaks.

OLIVER: Typical. (*he goes over to Alan, shouts in his ear*) Typical! Nothing less than I might have expected. I can't leave you alone for a second, can I, without you falling to pieces.

ALAN: (*raising his head*) No. Hopeless. I can't cry. Just like Gita. Except, she can't cry because she's too strong. Me - I can't spare my essential fluids. Don't worry, Oliver. I'm crying inside.

OLIVER: Don't over-exert yourself, not on my behalf.

ALAN: It's going to be difficult. I mean... it was always going to be difficult. But at least, since I came here... at least I've had someone to talk to.

OLIVER: Really. Self, self, self. Do you want to hear something really tragic? They haven't collected my body yet. From the airport. I'm in refrigerated storage, what do you think of that? Like a side of beef. Most undignified.

ALAN: I've never been very good at making friends. Nobody wanted to know me till I had something... concrete to give. Perhaps I wasn't worth knowing. But I could reel off the names of a dozen completely worthless people who've got... friends. Who've got love.

OLIVER: Why did every single one of our conversations eventually turn out to be about you? It's not as if you were ever particularly interesting.

ALAN: I remember... when my dad used to hit me, when I hadn't done anything. "It's not fair", I'd say. "The world isn't fair", he'd say. As if that excused him. Or the world.

OLIVER: Well, my father used to beat me as well. I mean, that's what fathers do.

ALAN: I saw him. This weekend. He looked at me like I was dirt. I wish... I wish I'd kicked his face in when I had the strength.

OLIVER: I'd heartily recommend it. A couple of lefts to the chin, then a right hook. He dropped like a sack of yams. Do you know what he called me? An abomination, because that's what it says in the Bible. Of course it also says that we should love our enemies, forgive the perceived sins of others, and judge not, that we be not judged, but why should one get bogged down in petty details?

ALAN:　　I always had too much respect, that was my trouble. I always figured that grown-ups knew best - my parents, school, the police. So, when I finally discovered that they were capable of lying, and cheating, and causing pain for no good reason... it hit me hard. Until... until I realised how piss-easy it was to get them back. "Come to me all ye who have been fucked up - and I will ease thy pain."

OLIVER:　　My father... he cried. When the call came. That his only son was dead. He cried. Oh, he wasn't crying for my eternal soul, for my pain, for the crushing of my spirit, the obliteration of my intellect. He was crying because of the rottenness of his seed, which could only produce two children - one a girl, and the other also less than male.

ALAN:　　I'm... I'm going to hell, aren't I? Wonder if I'll be able to tell the difference.

OLIVER: I'd gone back, for Christmas. Not long after those
hellish hours I'd spent in that cell, with you, as it
happened. My father... I had hit a policeman, so he
was indulgent. It wasn't something he approved of,
of course, but at least it showed that there was a
germ of manliness in me. He even talked to me,
about the family, about the business. We even... for
the first time, we got drunk together. Yes. We went
to a bar, which was owned by a friend of his. And
we drank all evening. I remember noticing how
many women there were, thinking how odd it was.
And then... there was a moment, a look which
passed between my father and his friend... and I was
ushered out of the bar-room and... "you look as
though you could do with a lie-down." Well, I was
in no fit state to argue. Another room, a smaller
room... a mattress, bare walls, no carpet... and this
girl... very young... too young. Small, a boyish
figure, small hips, small breasts, short hair...
obviously hand-picked. She took off my clothes,
and she massaged my temples, my shoulders, my
back... well, she worked her way down. And... my
body was playing tricks on me. And she turned me
onto my back, climbed on top of me, pulled me
inside her... it lasted... a very long time, I seem to
recall, through the mist... she didn't mind this, I
could tell. I flatter myself that I gave her pleasure.
Which would have been a novelty. I felt... almost

nothing. Eventually, the long moment passed. I became flaccid, remained... unresolved. It was only as she was dressing that I began to feel... resentful. And then... fearful. Since we had not taken prophylactic measures. "Don't worry about that, very clean girls here." I think I'd heard that coming from outside the room, but... I was hazy. Nothing clicked. Until... until months later, back in England, when I got the letter from my sister about my father being agitated about some girl who'd died... and I had the tests... and eventually, it became clear that I'd been infected. And my father had arranged the whole thing. Something poetic in that, I think.

ALAN: I wonder what your funeral's going to be like.

OLIVER: A quiet, shame-faced affair.

ALAN: Your sister... she'll cry. She cried when she was here, and you were looking relatively healthy, then. She looks pretty when she cries.

OLIVER: She cries easily, my sister. She's crying now.

ALAN: My sister won't cry, when I go. None of them will. Still, at least I know they'll turn up at the church. Quite a few people will, as a matter of fact. Give the public what they want, as the saying goes. Of course, the police will be there, to see who they can pick up. Or make a note of, to pick up at a later date. I've arranged everything, you see. The big day - the funeral, the party, the reading of the will... I've made sure everybody knows I've made my will. Took a lot of care over it. I think it gave my lawyers a good laugh.

OLIVER: I have nothing to leave anyone. Nothing of substance. Maybe... maybe some good memories for a number of people. Maybe people will think of me and smile.

ALAN: They were surprised at how much money I've got. "I think I'm in the wrong business, Mr McKenzie", one of them said. Joke. "We're in the same business", I said. That shut him up. I've split it neatly into thirds. One third to this place, one third to my sister, one third to the anti-Nazi movement. Nothing to do with conscience. It's all about practicality, see. Leaving something of value behind. To show that a worthless life needn't be a wasted life.

OLIVER: You surprise me. Pleasantly, for once.

ALAN: I'd love to be there. To see their faces. I'd love to be a fly on the wall.

OLIVER: Be careful what you wish for.

ALAN: My sister'll be shocked rigid. After all the ugly
words that have passed between us over the years.
But... I love her, you see. That's if I can love
anyone. I used to think... I used to tell myself it was
some weird, horrible sex thing. But only because
that was less embarrassing than the truth.

OLIVER: You working-class people - hours of amusement.

ALAN: I'm just trying to buy her forgiveness, of course.
Posthumously. I could never look her in the eyes
and do it. Actually, I could never look her in the
eyes full stop. Frightened of all the pain there.
Things I've done, things our parents have done,
things men have done... People never get what they
deserve. She deserves... someone who's going to
treat her like a lady. Instead of a whore, or a punch-
bag, or a baby machine. You should have met my
sister, Ollie. Not that you'd have liked her, not at
first. Very abrasive, my sister. But once you'd got
her trust... that was always her trouble, you see.
Trusting and mistrusting the wrong people. At
least, when she gets the money... it'll give her a bit
more choice. And the kids, of course. Her kids are
important. Not that I know them very well. She's

kept them away from me. She says I'm a bad
influence. I agree with her.

OLIVER: I never saw that photograph of your sister. Just as
well. I keep imagining the family resemblance.

He shudders.

ALAN: I've told her, she should bring them to see me, near
the end. Just so they know what to look forward to
if they follow my example. I'm sure Gita would
oblige with some of the more offensive details.

OLIVER: Ah, Gita. An angel. Her deathbed manner is very
impressive.

ALAN: I... I think... I think I love Gita as well. Or
perhaps... you know how it is. People under stress,
heightened sensitivity, spiritual tension, they label it
as whatever emotion seems appropriate. Fear, grief,
anger... love.

OLIVER: She's a beautiful person. A good person.

ALAN: If only I'd met someone like her ten years ago... no.
If I'd met someone like that ten years ago, if she
hadn't despised me, I wouldn't have had any
respect for her, I wouldn't have had any qualms

about dragging her down with me.

OLIVER: I don't believe that, Alan. Ten years ago... you were all potential. Just like me. We could have become... anything.

ALAN: I'd have dragged her down. And do you know what? I'd have enjoyed watching it happen.

OLIVER: No you wouldn't.

ALAN: No. No, I wouldn't. Still... she might have saved me. Or... or she might have given me the strength to save myself. Or the inclination. You see... I knew what I was doing.

OLIVER: Yes. You knew.

ALAN: Every druggie knows what they're doing. Or comes to know, sooner rather than later.

OLIVER: You're a fool, Alan.

ALAN: It was a joke, you see. Kind of. This sick bastard. Memo to my niece and nephew: "If you've ever going to run up a debt of several thousand quid, make sure it isn't with a sick bastard." I'd borrowed it to go in on a deal, you see. But it fell through.

Our wonderful Customs people stuck their oar in.
Occupational hazard. But Mr Sickbastard was
demanding repayment. Not necessarily in cash - a
hand would have done, or a testicle. I was about to
suggest the latter, after all, I didn't have much use
for mine. But then he whipped out his little
surprise. Had it in a fucking cool-box. "Or perhaps
you'd like to help me with a little experiment". Sick
bastard. He'd been saving it, ever since she died.
One of the women he ran. Another junkie. I'd
never had her. She was already too far gone. But he
took care of her. And he'd saved it. He'd saved her
works. "Tell you what", he said. "Help me with my
scientific research, and I'll cancel your little debt.
No - I'll turn your negative into a positive. Money-
wise, I mean." It was all about power, of course. He
was the main man, I was a pointless insect. The
money was nothing to him. He just wanted me on
my knees. He might as well as whipped his dick out
and made me do the business. But, frankly, the
needle was probably safer. Of course, he
misinterpreted the look on my face. He thought it
was fear. He laughed. But it wasn't fear. It was...
inspiration. I mean, what did I have to lose? I was a
drug addict, nobody loved me, I had a minus
amount of money... and it was always going to be
that way. The way his stupid mouth dropped open
when I said I'd do it. The way the colour drained

out of his face when I stuck the spike in...

OLIVER: Because you knew what was going to happen.

ALAN: Brilliant idea. It took away the fear, you see. It's amazing, the things you can achieve when the fear's gone. Giving yourself up to inevitability. To Fate. I mean, they were bound to get me, sooner or later. The police, or some other dealer, or a concerned parent. So, what do you do? You get yourself. You cut out the middle man, that's what you do. You take control. Do for yourself, before others do for you. As the Good Book says. Well, something like that.

OLIVER: No, Alan. That's not what you do. You acknowledge the bad things you've done, you stop doing them, and you atone.

ALAN: I know what you'd say, Oliver. You'd talk about... atonement, and shit like that. Leftover Jesus stuff. Which is all very well. Or it would be. Except - "love thy neighbour as thyself." Which means, that if you don't love yourself... who can judge you? And if nobody loves you... why should you judge yourself?

OLIVER: Because... because...

251

ALAN: See, at the back of my mind, I thought... maybe, if I'm dying, if I'm really dying... God will send someone to love me. The ultimate joke. The ultimate kindness. Whatever. Didn't work out that way, of course. Mr Sickbastard didn't manage to see out his experiment, either. Some other dealer blew his brains out a fortnight later. But he'd already given me the money, so that was alright. And I used it wisely. Immorally, but wisely.

OLIVER: You made a terrible mistake.

ALAN: I understand everything, you see, Oliver. I understand everything in my life. I figured out the awful truth about myself. I figured out why I didn't feel worse about the things I did, why I didn't feel guilty about being... a traitor. I'm... it's like... in the Bible... did you ever think what would have happened if Judas Iscariot hadn't betrayed Christ? Nothing. Nothing would have happened. You see, some people have to be bad, in order that others can be seen to be good. Some people have to make terrible mistakes in order that others can learn from these mistakes. And some people have to remain unloved, so that those who are loved can look, and learn, and appreciate what they have. This is the truth. The truth has set me free.

Alan sighs, gets to his feet. Oliver shakes his head, sadly.

OLIVER: That's the most ridiculous thing I've ever heard.

ALAN: Anyway - best go check out my new CD collection. Make the most of it, while I've got the chance.

He starts to leave.

OLIVER: You are an idiot! A fool! An imbecile! You have got shit for brains! You know nothing, you deserve nothing, you are nothing!

Alan stops, chuckles, looks around the room.

ALAN: I can almost hear you, Ollie. That annoying habit you had. Telling me things I already knew. "You are an appalling person." Except... except it was too late then, and it's definitely too late now.

He starts to leave. Oliver blocks his path. Alan stops dead, not quite knowing why.

OLIVER: You don't really think you're going to be allowed to get away with all this crap, do you? No. Of course you don't. There's still time, you know. Time for you to save yourself. You do know what you have to do, don't you? Don't you?

ALAN: Mind you, though... maybe... maybe there is time.
Time to... to make Gita love me. That's the thing I
want most in the world. You see, it was easy for her
to love you, Ollie. You were on the same
wavelength, you know, all that university shit. Plus
you weren't exactly a threat. Not lately, anyway.
But me - I'm an entirely different proposition. Yes.
That's it. I'm damned if I'm going to die alone.
Alone inside. I'm going to make her love me. Yes.
So when I'm slipping away, and she's holding my
hand... there'll be tears in her eyes. Real, loving
tears. Yeah. How's that for a final challenge, eh?
How's that for the labours of Hercules? I'll make
you so proud of me, Ollie, old son. You'll see.

He leaves.

OLIVER: Yes, well - it's a start.

He smiles to himself.

Slow Blackout.

Music - Coltrane's "Naima".

Killing Kangaroos
Roger Williams

Killing Kangaroos was premiered in Cardiff in October 1999 before going on to play Newport and Swansea. It had previously been featured at the Australian National Playwrights' conference in Canberra. In Wales it had the following cast:

RHODRI - Richard Norton

MEGAN - Valmai Jones

RAY - Stan Pretty

GWEN - Lucinda Cowden

GETHIN - Huw Davies

EMMA - Shelley Miranda Barrett

CERI - Martin Cole

MAN - Kristian Zgorzelskii

Director - Jeff Teare

Designer - Carolyn Willitts

Lighting design - Chris Davies

Dramaturg - Rachel Hennessy

Production Manager - Giles Parbery

Stage Manager - Ian Buchanan

Characters

It is important to note that the role of CERI must be played by a black actor.

GETHIN	24 year-old - Welsh
EMMA	24 year-old - Welsh
CERI	25 year-old - Welsh

MEGAN	55 year-old Australian - born in Wales 1943
RAY	mid-50s - Australian
GWEN	29 year-old - Australian
RHODRI	22 year-old - Australian

The action is set in Sydney, Australia, in the summer of 1999.

Location

The setting is the living room of a large house in the affluent suburb of North Sydney. Like so many Australian homes of its era it was designed to be open-plan. The living room takes up most of the stage but upstage right is the kitchen area complete with breakfast bar. The living room is dominated by a large sofa (lounge) just left of centre.

Along the back wall are two glass sliding doors which lead out towards the terrace. This is one of the principal entry points. Turning stage-left through these doors characters can walk down to the swimming pool, and turning stage-right they can walk towards the driveway. Visible through these doors are a variety of shrubs and small plants, but the ground is paved. On stage right is a door leading to the hall and the outside world. Stage left there is an opening (no door) that leads to the rest of the house.

This could be the home of any middle-class Australian soap family. It is a realistic looking Australian house which has been sanitised by the design department of a television company. This world isn't real, and towards the end of the play its inadequacies as a real place should become apparent in order to reflect the characters' discovery that their own existence is both frangible and flawed. The physical environment should somehow reflect the changes they have undertaken.

Scene Breakdown

ACT ONE	Scene One	Monday - late morning
	Scene Two	Tuesday - late morning
	Scene Three	Wednesday - very early morning (dark outside)
	Scene Four	Thursday - evening
ACT TWO	Scene One	Friday - morning
	Scene Two	Saturday - afternoon
	Scene Three	Sunday - very early morning (dark outside)
	Scene Four	Wednesday - afternoon

Act One - Scene One

*In darkness we hear a sudden burst of loud music. It should be
          something modern and immediate, for example
          'Right Here, Right Now' by Fat Boy Slim. The lights
          rise to reveal an empty room, before RHODRI
          appears behind the sliding glass doors at the rear of the
          stage wearing swimming goggles over his eyes, and a
          pair of Speedos. He has just emerged from the
          swimming pool and is soaking wet. He waits outside,
          removes his goggles, slides the door open and steps
          inside. RHODRI crosses to the cd player and starts
          'Right Here, Right Now' by Fat Boy Slim (This
          crashes in over the previous track). He then walks to
          the kitchen where he opens the fridge, and removes a
          carton of milk. He finds a bowl and a box of
          cornflakes on the counter, and makes himself some
          cereal. He takes his breakfast over to the sofa, and
          begins to eat the cereal as though he hasn't seen food in
          days. Beat. From behind the glass doors Megan
          appears. She has just returned from the supermarket
          and is awkwardly carrying a clutch of bulging carrier
          bags. MEGAN comes inside and drops the bags to the
          floor. The music fades.*

MEGAN   Home. Thank God. There've been times today when
              I thought I'd never make it.

RHODRI   Hassles?

MEGAN   You could say that. The air-con's gone in the
              Holden, and it's just taken me an hour, one hour, to
              get from Coles to here.

RHODRI   You should've taken the handbrake off.

MEGAN crosses to the kitchen.

MEGAN   The traffic's murder, Rhodri. Cars piled up past the
              on-ramp, two lanes closed, and everything down to a
              crawl. God knows what anyone with a brain was
              doing trying to cross that freeway. They're pushing a
              hundred and ten along there.

RHODRI   And the rest.

MEGAN   He must've gotten half way and been trying to find a
              gap he could slip through when it clonked him. One
              car spun onto the verge, and three others have gone
              the same way. Havoc doesn't even begin to describe
              it. I don't know how I'm going to get everything
              done by two now.

RHODRI   Take it easy Mum. You don't want to bust a gut.

MEGAN   'Seen your father this morning?

RHODRI shakes his head. He is still eating.

MEGAN   He's probably stuck in the jam. That'll put a smile on his face.

RHODRI   You haven't got to make such a fuss, you know?

MEGAN   They've come a long way and I want everything to be ready.

RHODRI   I thought you said they were getting the bus up from Wagga?

MEGAN   You know what I mean. I don't want them thinking they've come to a pig sty.

RHODRI   They're backpackers Mum. They're used to squalor.

MEGAN   Talking of which, have you cleaned your room yet?

RHODRI   Nah. Been swimming.

MEGAN   Dressed like that I should hope so too.

RHODRI   Hit two minutes forty today.

MEGAN   Time you spend in that pool I'm surprised you don't develop webbed feet.

RHODRI   Be back in the squad at this rate, no worries.

MEGAN   And gills. So you haven't seen your sister either then?

RHODRI   Saw her Friday. Racing out the house in a very short skirt, with a very large bottle of champagne tucked under her arm.

MEGAN   Don't suppose she said where she was going?

RHODRI   Told me she'd see us in the morning.

MEGAN   Yes, but she didn't mean Monday morning, did she Rhodri?

RHODRI   Gwen's twenty-nine Mum. Carries a pepper spray. If there's been any trouble, odds on she started it.

MEGAN   I just hope your father doesn't find out. He'll blow his top if he thinks she's been raging all weekend long.

RHODRI   Kaboom!

MEGAN   Will you please go and sort out your room?

RHODRI   I always get the shitty end of the stick. Gwen'd chuck
              a tanty if you told her she had to give her bed up for
              a stranger. Have a huge spack and start breaking
              furniture.

MEGAN   Why d'you think we didn't?

RHODRI   It's insane. You're rolling out the red carpet and
              you've never even met them.

MEGAN   Gethin's family Rhodri. I want things to be right.

RHODRI   Gethin? Another Welsh name you can't help saying
              without bringing up phlegm.

MEGAN   Don't be crude.

RHODRI   Almost as nice as Rhodri.

MEGAN   There's nothing wrong with Rhodri.

RHODRI   Not if you're from deepest darkest Wales perhaps,
              but when it's your first day at Crow's Nest High and
              everyone's calling you Row Dry, the novelty value
              soon wears off.

MEGAN   Room. Clean. Now.

RHODRI   Alright, alright. I'm on my way.

MEGAN   If only you moved as fast on your feet as you did in the water I'd be a happy woman. And I mean clean this time Rhodri. Don't just kick your socks under the bed and hope they disappear. Because given time they'll start walking out by themselves. Alright?

As MEGAN delivers the last line she places her hand on RHODRI's head to ruffle his hair and realises that he's still wet.

MEGAN   Aw, Rhodri! No! How many times? Up. Come on.

RHODRI gets up and MEGAN inspects the sofa.

MEGAN   It's soaking!

RHODRI   I've been swimming.

MEGAN   I know you've been swimming, but do you have to use my sofa to do dry yourself off on when you're finished?

RHODRI   I forgot.

MEGAN   And I thought only goldfish had a three second memory.

RHODRI   I'm sorry, alright?

MEGAN   Go on. Upstairs. You know the routine well enough by now.

RHODRI   I bet Ian Thorpe doesn't get bullied like this.

MEGAN   And try not to drip any water on my carpets.

RHODRI exits stage left. MEGAN pats her side pocket, and finds a handful of scrunched up carrier bags which she distantly remembers putting there.

MEGAN   The day I actually remember to use the bags I've taken with me to the supermarket will be the day I drop dead from shock.

RAY enters through the glass doors. He is smartly dressed, carries a briefcase and a clutch of fat document wallets.

MEGAN   We thought you'd got lost.

RAY   Have you seen the state of that freeway? Jesus. Looks like a bloody war zone. It's taken me an age to get back from the city, and all because some stupid kid fancies himself as a flipping dare devil. Some people just go looking for trouble, don't they?

MEGAN   I thought it was an accident.

RAY   Nah. Bloody idiot was running across the road on purpose love. Trying to impress his mates.

MEGAN   How d'you know that?

RAY   'Wound down the window and asked one of the cops. Lebanese boy, he reckoned. On his way to school this morning takes a bet from one of his pals he can run across the freeway and back in less than sixty seconds. 'Course, it all turns nasty when he sees a Honda Civic coming at him doing eighty. The ambos were scraping up what was left when I eventually drove past. And all for twenty bucks.

MEGAN   Terrible isn't it?

RAY   You're telling me. Traffic's going to be buggered for hours now.

MEGAN   Did you talk to Steve?

RAY   Nah, he's off crook. Saw some other bloke. Yan? Yim?

MEGAN   Yim? What's that? Korean?

RAY   I dunno. 'Didn't ask him where he goes for his holidays.

MEGAN   Ray.

RAY   Mee-gan, I saw this Asian guy, he read the proposal, played with his computer, smiled a smile, and said the bank'd be in touch.

MEGAN   You didn't get an answer?

RAY   He had to show it to the blokes upstairs. Procedure. Reckon he's only been in the job two minutes.

MEGAN   Do you think they'll give it to us though?

RAY   Look love, they can see it's a good strategy. They're not brain dead.

MEGAN   So Mr. Yim's going to call when they've made a decision, is he?

RAY   He'll probably be running the place by the end of the week. Get one of his minions to do it.

MEGAN   Ray!

RAY   What? When these Asians get a foot-hold they don't let go until they've climbed to the top. You know that as well as me.

MEGAN   Just watch yourself when Gethin gets here. I don't want him going home calling you racist with all your talk.

RAY   Look, if your rellos turned up here this arvo and said, "G'day Ray. Guess what mate? We're not going home after all now. We like the weather you blokes get down here, your beaches and that, so we're going to stay put," I'd say the same to them. I'd drive them to the airport and stick them on the first plane back to England. A rule's a rule love, and it goes for everyone. Crack down on immigration, close the doors, and sort ourselves out. There's no shame in that.

MEGAN   Well, when the money does come through can you make certain everything runs smoothly this time please?

RAY   It was a simple mistake.

MEGAN   An expensive mistake.

RAY   Which won't happen again. Even Yim said it was bad luck. Don't worry, eh? She'll be right.

MEGAN   I hope so. I've enough on my plate this week without re-living that particular drama.

RAY   What time are they arriving?

MEGAN   Two o'clock. Doesn't anyone around here remember anything? And when they come through that door I want the whole family waiting to welcome them, alright? Everyone.

RAY   Did I say I wasn't going to be here? Did I? Nah, I want to meet this nephew of yours.

MEGAN   Ours.

RAY   Sounds like the perfect child from what I've heard. A responsible teacher. Maybe some of it'll rub off on Gwen.

MEGAN   You shouldn't wind her up, Ray.

RAY   When she moved out of home eight years ago I wasn't banking on her coming back.

MEGAN   It's not easy finding work in her line. You know that.

RAY   And it's bloody impossible if you sit around doing bugger all about it. 'Talk to her these days you'd be forgiven for thinking she's taken early retirement.

MEGAN   Give her time.

RAY   It's not time Gwen needs. It's a kick up the arse. She should be out there. Meeting producers, doing the rounds, sending off her CV. And now that she's got shot of that waster once and for all, there's no excuse, is there? I only want what's best for her Meegan. I want to see her safe, and settled.

MEGAN hands him a duster and can of polish.

MEGAN   Well, while you're waiting you can start on the front room.

RAY   Opportunities like that don't come along twice in a lifetime. Not unless you go after them.

RHODRI comes back on carrying a hairdryer.

MEGAN   Ray, we're going to make a good impression if it kills me. And at this rate it probably will.

RHODRI   Roped you in too has she Dad?

RAY   Don't reckon anyone's safe, mate. I haven't seen your mother this excited since The Bee Gees announced they were playing Stadium Australia.

RHODRI   Yeah, I'm surprised she hasn't made a little sign to wave at them when the bus pulls in.

RAY   "Welshies walk this way!"

RHODRI   "Hello, my name is Mee-gan," and a little red arrow pointing up at her face.

MEGAN   Off!

RAY exits. MEGAN pulls on a pair of rubber gloves as if she were going into surgery. She forages in the cupboard and finds a toilet brush. RHODRI goes back to the sofa.

RHODRI   I don't believe you're making me do this again. It was just a bit of water.

MEGAN   Simple science lesson for you Rhodri. Wet skin. Dry towel. Rub. The sooner you grasp that principle the better off we'll all...

RHODRI switches on the hair dryer deliberately cutting off

MEGAN's last line. He continues to dry the sofa. MEGAN exits stage left. RHODRI plays with the hair dryer; shaking it around. Pause. GWEN enters through the glass doors at the back of the stage. She is looking rough; her hair is a mess and she is wearing dark glasses. GWEN tries to sneak off stage left without being noticed but RHODRI switches off the hair dryer, and GWEN freezes.

RHODRI Busted!

GWEN Sorry? Did somebody fart?

RHODRI Mum's looking for you. Reckon she thought you were going to turn up in a body bag on 'Australia's Most Wanted'.

GWEN Jesus.

RHODRI But then we realised that that's a TV show. Which is the last place we'd see you nowadays, eh?

GWEN Go drown yourself.

GWEN pours herself some orange juice.

RHODRI Jeez Gwen, ratshit's looked better.

GWEN Don't be a sook all your life, Rod. I'm sick. I've been drinking champagne since Friday and the only reason

I stopped was because they ran out. So shut up, will you?

RHODRI   Where d'you go?

GWEN   Sinitta's party at the TV station, then we kicked on to a club in Cockle Bay, but the cab I just came home in picked me up on Darling Street. Don't know how I got there, and don't think I want to.

RHODRI   The old man's home.

GWEN   Full of good news this morning, aren't you?

RHODRI   'Been busy at work. Doesn't know you've been out.

GWEN   And he's not going to either, is he Rod? Is that my hair dryer?

RHODRI   Yeah. Mum finally flipped and declared war on dirt. The guests are arriving today.

GWEN   Shit. Why can't they stay in a hotel like normal people?

RHODRI   Because, as Mum'll remind you when she gets a chance, they're family.

GWEN   So their not just cheap skate students looking for a free lunch then? Christ, I hate back packers. They're so... ferral.

RHODRI   Given your unusually good mood this morning, I take it nobody came up with an offer of a job at this party you went to?

GWEN   Huh, they don't want a bar of you unless you've got your face splattered all over the tabloids. And those rags aren't interested unless you're rooting Australia's richest man, or having a seedy affair with a four foot midget and his ten inch cock. Unfortunately brother, I don't know anyone who fits the bill.

RHODRI   How tall d'you say he'd have to be again?

GWEN   Christ, what I'd do for a movie, a record deal, anything to get me out of this place and shut Ray up.

RHODRI   You'll be lucky.

GWEN   I've just got to convince them I'm not a washed up soap star who'd be better off giving in, moving to Dubbo, and opening a fish 'n' chip shop. I need to remind the bastards that I'm still alive.

RHODRI   Even though you look half dead.

MEGAN re-enters stage-left.

MEGAN   Back then are you? You do remember what day it is today, don't you Gwen?

GWEN   Sorry. I left the city hours ago, but there's been a huge accident down on the freeway and nothing's moving.

MEGAN   Did you hear how it happened?

GWEN   Yeah, what a bunch of bastards. They should hang them up by the balls if you ask me.

MEGAN   Who?

GWEN   The ones who made him do it.

MEGAN   Nobody made him do it Gwen. It was a bet.

GWEN   Bullshit. Who told you that?

MEGAN   Your father. The boy bet his friends twenty dollars he could dodge the cars on the freeway.

GWEN   Nah, Mum. Gang of yobbos took the poor bastard down there and made him run it.

MEGAN   Come off it Gwen. How could you make someone do that unless they really wanted to?

GWEN   With a knife. They were gonna stick it in him if he didn't.

RAY enters stage right with the cleaning materials and wearing an apron.

RAY   Well, well. Surfaced at last, have you?

GWEN   Nice outfit Ray. Is that what you're wearing to Mardi Gras?

RAY   Don't you know we've got guests coming today?

RHODRI   How could we forget?

MEGAN   And if we all get a shift on we might get this place looking half decent by the time they arrive, yes? Rhodri, clear those magazines away. Ray, I want to see that duster in action please, and Gwen, start laying the food out on the brekkie bar. It's all ready. Just peel off the Glad Wrap.

GWEN   Great. Now I'm the hired help.

GWEN reluctantly goes to the fridge and starts to bring out the plates of sandwiches which she places on the breakfast bar. RHODRI starts to sort through the magazines, and RAY half-heartedly dusts.

MEGAN   Touch wood it'll all be in shape by two.

GWEN   'Wish they'd make their minds up. First of all it's two o'clock, then it's eleven, and now it's two again. Are they pulling the piss, or what?

MEGAN   No no, it's always been two o'clock Gwen. Gethin wrote last week and told me it was two o'clock.

GWEN   Didn't you get the message then?

RAY   What message?

GWEN   They called Friday. Said they were getting an earlier bus. It's on the pad.

RAY goes off right to get the message pad.

MEGAN   I didn't see a message.

GWEN   Well, I wrote it down!

RHODRI   Smells like trouble.

MEGAN takes the pad from RAY and reads the message. She squints. GWEN snatches the pad back.

GWEN   "Friday. Visitors arriving at eleven."

MEGAN   And what language is that supposed to be in?

GWEN   It's not my fault you haven't got an answering machine.

RHODRI   Red alert. Red alert.

MEGAN   What time is it now Ray?

RAY   Twelve.

MEGAN   Oh God, they're here, they've arrived.

RHODRI   They arrived over an hour ago.

MEGAN   I hope they've waited. D'you think they've waited?

RHODRI   Dunno. An hour's a long time to hang around.

RAY   Rod. Shut up mate.

MEGAN   You see Gwen. This is what happens when you stay out three nights running and don't come home until the last minute, isn't it?

RAY   She what!

GWEN   I was in a rush. I couldn't find a pen.

MEGAN   I thought it was just a lipstick smudge.

GWEN   Well I wasn't going to waste my eyeliner!

MEGAN   I'll have to make my way over there now and hope
               they've had enough sense to stay put.

RHODRI   Well, if the traffic's as screwed as everyone says it is
               they won't have gone very far.

RAY   Rhodri!

MEGAN   'Need to change. Pull a brush through my hair.

RAY   Don't panic. Nobody is going to panic.

GWEN   Too right.

MEGAN   Will you sort this mess out Ray? Make it look tidy at
               least?

RAY   'Course.

MEGAN   Oh God, what must they be thinking?

MEGAN hurries off left to change.

RAY   I thought you didn't have any money.

GWEN   Here we go.

RAY   So how can you afford to go gallivanting then, eh?

GWEN   Got lucky on a sratchy.

RAY   Gwen!

GWEN   Blake paid. He wanted me to go out and enjoy myself, so Blake said he'd shout me.

RAY   Your Abo mate?

GWEN   Don't say that.

RAY   Why not?

GWEN   It's offensive.

RAY   Christ, it's getting so that you can't say anything these days without it offending someone or other.

What would you rather I called him then? Black? Non-white? Indigenous?

GWEN   Have you been a wanker all your life Ray, or is it something that happened late in life?

RAY   Oh, and I suppose that wasn't meant to be offensive, was it?

GWEN   Jeez you're an arse hole.

RAY   And what does this Blake do for a living?

GWEN   He's an artist.

RAY   Another bludger.

GWEN   Oh, piss off.

RAY   My tax dollars, Gwen. No wonder this country's buggered.

GWEN   You're full of shit Ray. You really are.

RAY   I am, am I?

GWEN   Yeah. And most of it's coming out your mouth.

MEGAN enter in a new outfit..

MEGAN   God, if I had a brain I sometimes think I'd be dangerous, you know?

MEGAN searches for her keys.

RAY   It's about time you took a long hard look at yourself, Gwen. You're nearly thirty.

GWEN   Twenty-nine, thank you.

RAY   You'll have to settle down sooner or later. You can't keep running around like this.

MEGAN   I won't get there before dark at this rate.

GWEN has continued unpacking the sandwiches in silence. RAY is cleaning.

MEGAN   Ray, you seen my keys?

RAY   Sorry love.

MEGAN   I haven't even met them and already it's all gone horribly wrong.

RHODRI   Yeah. Shocking, isn't it?

GWEN is glaring at one plate of sandwiches in particular.

GWEN   Mum? What've you put in these sangers?

MEGAN comes over and looks.

MEGAN   Avocado and cottage cheese, love. Why?

GWEN   'Thought so.

GWEN turns to the sink and prepares to throw up.

MEGAN   Oh God. Not in the bowl!

RAY   And she reckons she's old enough to look after
               herself.

*MEGAN runs to the sink and lifts out the washing up bowl before
GWEN actually vomits.*

RHODRI   Cool.

GWEN vomits. MEGAN tries to comfort her.

RAY   Just get on with it Rod.

MEGAN   You've got to learn to say when enough is enough

Gwen.

RAY   That's her trouble. It never will be.

RHODRI turns his attention back to the hair dryer, switches it on, and continues to dry the settee. RAY carries on dusting. MEGAN supports GWEN at the sink. Whilst this activity is going on, GETHIN, CERI and EMMA appear behind the glass doors at the rear of the stage. They look in and after a moment decide to come inside. They are carrying large heavy backpacks. They stand at the door waiting to be noticed. RAY is the first to spot them, then GWEN who turns away from the sink, then MEGAN, and finally RHODRI, who looks up. After a pause he switches off the hair dryer. GETHIN, CERI and EMMA enter the room. The characters look at one another not sure what to say next. Silence.

CERI   Alright? Not disturbing anything, are we?

Pause. 'Soap Moment'. Music. Blackout.

Act One - Scene Two

The next day - Tuesday. Lights rise to reveal GETHIN standing centre looking around for someone. He is wearing baggy swim-shorts, and has a towel draped over his shoulder. Bored, he pulls on his goggles, drops and mimes the breast stroke. MEGAN enters through the sliding glass doors carrying an audio cassette that has clearly seen better days. GETHIN turns and sees her - goggles and all.

MEGAN   Barry, Robin and Maurice. Melted. 'Leave anything on the dashboard in this heat and it might as well be chocolate. 'Least Gwen'll be chuffed. To hear her talking you'd think the Bee Gees had done her personal harm. 'Going for a swim, Gethin?

GETHIN   O'n i'n gob'ith'o 'se Rhodri'n mynd 'da fi. Ble ma' fe?
Yeah, I was hoping Rhodri could show me the way. Where is he?

MEGAN   Taken the others on a tour.

GETHIN   Dyle chi wedi diluno fi.
Oh, you should've woken me.

MEGAN   I wanted to, but the others spoilt my fun. Said you needed the rest. Emma was bursting with excitement over breakfast, wanted to look at the Opera House.

You can just about see the roof from the wharf, if you don't mind standing on the wall and stretching your neck to the left a bit. Can I get you some breakfast Gethin?

GETHIN   'Mond sudd oren, diolch.
Erm, just an orange juice thanks.

MEGAN   Nothing else?

GETHIN   Nah. Might as well wait for lunch now.

MEGAN heads to the kitchen and leaves the cassette on the breakfast bar as she goes. She pours GETHIN a glass of fruit juice from the fridge.

MEGAN   After all that time spent sleeping in hostels it must be a change for you to have your own room.

GETHIN   Yeah, it's a luxury not to be sharing a dorm with someone who snores, or a sweaty stranger in need of a good bath.

MEGAN   Mind you, you've been places most Australians never get to see. We've all been to Bali, but who's ever been to Birdsville? You'll have to let me see the photos some time.

GETHIN   Sure. I've got some others in my room for you too. Mum sent them over. You and her when you were little.

MEGAN   Good God. Artefacts.

GETHIN   I'll fetch them if you like. We can go through them now.

MEGAN   There's no rush Gethin. They've kept this long, they'll keep a few hours more.

CERI enters through the sliding glass doors.

MEGAN   The wanderers return. Had enough, have you?

CERI   Yeah. Emma's down the pool with Rhodri. *(To Gethin)* Morning mate.

GETHIN   Morning.

CERI   I'm shattered

MEGAN   Drink Ceri?

CERI   Bit early isn't it, Mrs. H?

MEGAN   Of orange juice.

CERI   Straight? That'd be very nice thank you.

GETHIN   Enjoy your walk?

CERI   Yeah, we did. Rhodri's a laugh, isn't he?

GETHIN   I wouldn't know.

MEGAN gives him the drink.

CERI   Ta. Just what I needed.

MEGAN   Where did he take you in the end?

CERI   Where didn't he? I feel like a thoroughbred
             Sydneysider now thanks to Rhodri. That boy must
             have Duracell batteries.

MEGAN   He's very fit. Does a lot of swimming.

CERI   Three hours training a day, he said. Makes me tired
             just thinking about it.

MEGAN   He's been swimming since he was a boy.
             Represented the state one year.

CERI   Wow, that's impressive. Isn't that impressive Geth?

MEGAN   His Dad's always encouraged him.

CERI   And it's obviously paid off.

CERI drains his glass.

CERI   Chance of another?

MEGAN   Oh, 'course.

MEGAN takes the glass and goes to the kitchen to pour another glass of orange juice.

GETHIN   Creep.

CERI   Get a life Gethin.

MEGAN returns.

MEGAN   By the way, Vanessa called earlier. She was wondering if you'd had a chance to consider her offer.

GETHIN   What's this?

MEGAN   Vanessa Pappos, chair of Sydney Welsh Society, has asked Ceri to give us a talk. About his studies.

GETHIN   Sydney Welsh Society?

MEGAN   SWS. Vanessa was very excited when she heard about your work Ceri, your M.A., and now a doctorate. Said her two brain cells'd've trouble struggling with one of those.

CERI   Oh, I don't know. My two manage alright.

GETHIN   When he can find them.

CERI   I thought I might give a brief lecture on the portrayal of the Welsh in television and film.

GETHIN   Very brief.

CERI   Expressions of cultural identity as perceived on the small and big screens, and the mythologies these have given rise to. That's what I did my M.A. on.

MEGAN   Just don't make it too difficult's what I'd say. We're not all academics and to be honest, some of the older ones wouldn't be able to keep up.

CERI   But you're all ex-pats, are you?

MEGAN   Or descended from Welsh stock. Except Mrs. Wong.

She's Chinese. Her husband died last year and we try to include her best we can. You won't believe how excited Vanessa was to find out there were real live Welsh people in the area. She misses Wales terribly.

GETHIN   Why? When did she move to Sydney?

MEGAN   Eighty-five.

CERI   Where from?

MEGAN   Brisbane.

GETHIN   Oh. So, she's not Welsh then?

MEGAN   Welsh-Australian. Like Rolf Harris. Her grandmother was from Port Talbot.

CERI   Really? I'm surprised she emigrated.

MEGAN   And her great great grandfather was from Pembrokeshire. Had a free passage over, the lot.

CERI   Oh yeah. What did he do to deserve that?

MEGAN   Arson. Burnt down his neighbour's hay stack on Monday, transported by the end of the week. I'm sure she'll tell you the story herself when you meet her. Trust me. She's got a mouth the size of Sydney Harbour.

MEGAN finds the laundry basket on the breakfast bar, and exits stage left.

GETHIN glares at CERI.

GETHIN   Thanks for this morning Ceri.

CERI   You're welcome.

GETHIN   How much longer are you and Emma going to keep this up?

CERI   What?

GETHIN   Freezing me out? Ignoring me? It's pathetic Ceri.

CERI   And what you've been doing isn't I suppose?

GETHIN stares at him, turns, and exits stage right towards the front door. CERI sits down and flicks through the TV guide. EMMA and RHODRI appear behind the sliding doors and come in.

CERI   You know, I'll never get over the shock of coming to this country and discovering you only get 'Neighbours' once a day. It's criminal.

RHODRI   Soap opera junkie are you, mate?

EMMA   Doesn't stop at soap opera. This one'll watch
               anything that's on.

RHODRI   You should have a talk to my sister then. You know
               she was in one of those soapies for three years, don't
               you?

EMMA   Does he ever. That's all he's talked about since we
               left home. "D'you think it'd be naff if I asked Gwen
               for a signed photo? D'you think she'd have her
               picture taken with me? Gwen Seghuh, nah, nah,
               bloody nah, nah."

CERI   I'm not that bad.

EMMA   How come she changed her name anyway? Your
               surname's Hughes.

CERI   It's quite a common name Emma. It's obvious there
               must've been two actresses called Gwen Hughes
               working in Australia, and she was forced to assume a
               new moniker.

EMMA   Hey! Listen to the Media Studies expert.

RHODRI   It sounded boring. That's why she changed it. Jeez, there were sparks flying the day Dad caught on. He was mad as a cut snake.

EMMA   But why Seghuh?

RHODRI   Hughes. Spelt backwards. She did it when she got the job on Shellcove.

CERI   But she's left Shellcove Bay now, hasn't she?

RHODRI   Yep, got pushed off the back of a boat by a jealous ex-lover thirty k's out at sea. "The most dramatic season finale ever," according to TV Week.

EMMA   And she drowned?

RHODRI   Nah, the sharks got her. It's a great episode. We've got it on tape if you want to see it.

Sudden silence. RHODRI becomes uncomfortable.

RHODRI   What? What's wrong?

CERI   Cheers mate. I was wondering what happened.

EMMA   The BBC's a year behind. Ceri hasn't seen that episode yet.

CERI   She was just getting married to Derek when we left.

RHODRI   Oh well that didn't last. He went off with Alex the car mechanic.

CERI   You're one of those annoying bastards who enjoys spoiling the punch-line of a good joke, one of those anal retentives who reads the last chapter of a novel before he starts on the first. You ruin everything!

CERI exits up centre.

RHODRI   He's good value, isn't he?

EMMA   Yeah, see how much fun you could have if you came out with us tonight.

RHODRI   I dunno.

EMMA   Oh come on. It'd be a laugh. Besides, we need someone who can show us the way.

RHODRI   Night-clubs aren't my thing Emma.

EMMA   You said you've only been once.

RHODRI   I don't dance.

EMMA   So stand at the bar with a beer in your hand. Please?

RHODRI   I'll think about it.

EMMA   Great. We'll leave about nine.

RHODRI   Emma!

EMMA   What? You're thinking about it, and by nine o'clock you'll have realised what a fantastic idea it is and be sitting next to me and Ceri on the train into town.

RHODRI   Are you always so full on?

EMMA   When I want something bad enough, yeah.

RHODRI   What about Gethin? Won't he be coming?

EMMA   Not if we can help it, no.

RHODRI   I thought he was your boyfriend.

EMMA   He was. We split up.

RHODRI   When?

EMMA   Six months ago. Perth airport, the baggage carousel.

We'd just arrived in the country, and he'd pulled my back-pack off the conveyor belt. I told him that I didn't want to trek around Australia holding his sweaty little hand after all, and that I wanted to kill the relationship.

RHODRI   Jeez.

EMMA   I'd been thinking about it for a while. Since we took off from Heathrow actually. It was ten hours into the flight when I finally realised I didn't love him anymore. Gethin was fast asleep. Head slumped to one side. Dribble running down the corner of his mouth. I looked at him and thought, "I don't need this in my life. It's making me miserable." 'Course, when we stepped into the arrival hall and saw those great big signs they've got in customs I knew it was an omen. "Declare it, or dump it." Didn't have a lot of choice really, did I?

RHODRI   How did he take it?

EMMA   Not too bad considering. Naturally he was disappointed, upset even. But he should've seen it coming a mile off. Things had been turning sour for ages.

RHODRI   Christ.

EMMA   By the time we were headed for Adelaide he'd
                bucked up. Stopped crying at least.

RHODRI   He's alright now, but?

EMMA   Don't know. He's been a bit of a prick all holiday so
                I've kept my distance.

RHODRI   Why? What's he been doing?

EMMA   Telling tales. Inventing little stories just to shit stir.
                You know the type of thing, telling Ceri I thought
                he was a boring bastard, and telling me Ceri thought
                I was a greedy heartless bitch. Usual sort of stuff. It
                was only when Gethin pissed us both off
                simultaneously in Darwin, and we started
                complaining about him to one another that the
                penny dropped. Gethin can be pretty vindictive when
                he wants to be I promise you.

EMMA finds the cassette on the breakfast bar.

EMMA   What's this?

RHODRI takes a look.

RHODRI   The Bee Gees' "Greatest Hits".

EMMA   'Didn't think they had any.

RHODRI   Mum's mad on them. She must've left it on the dash again and it melted. That's the second she's cooked this month.

GETHIN enters.

GETHIN   What are you two up to, then? Making plans for this afternoon?

EMMA   This evening actually.

GETHIN   D'you have a nice morning?

EMMA   Lovely thanks. Your cousin here's been the perfect host.

GETHIN   Is that right?

Awkward pause.

RHODRI   Erm, I'd better go and see what Ceri's up to. Make sure he hasn't fallen in, hey?

EMMA   Good idea. I'll catch you up.

RHODRI exits up centre.

GETHIN   Playing your games again, Emma?

EMMA   I don't know what you're talking about.

GETHIN   Don't mess with these people. They're my family.

EMMA   As if you'd let us forget it. And what was all that crap
               you were spouting about your aunty? She looks
               alright to me.

GETHIN   You know the story.

EMMA   I should do. I've heard it enough times.

GETHIN   She was devastated.

EMMA   They were engaged Gethin. She was bound to be
               upset.

GETHIN   Mum didn't know what she'd be like. Be sensitive,
               she said. Take things easy.

EMMA   Oh Gethin, stop making such a fuss, will you? She's
               fine. Fine. Like always, you just love a good drama.

MEGAN enters stage-left.

MEGAN   Off out again? Might as well make the most of the sunshine.

EMMA   Rhodri promised to show me his backstroke.

GETHIN   Yeah, wants to take us swimming. All three of us. Doesn't he, Em?

EMMA and GETHIN exit.

MEGAN   Oh! Make sure he's got his towel then please!

MEGAN goes into the kitchen and RAY enters from the stage right entrance a moment later. He lays his briefcase down. RAY's smiling widely. MEGAN looks at him.

MEGAN   Well?

RAY laughs.

MEGAN   You should've phoned!

RAY pulls MEGAN into an embrace. He stops smiling (unseen by Megan) – 'Soap Moment'. Blackout.

Act One - Scene Three

Very early the following morning - Wednesday. It is dark outside. Music fades. Lights rise to reveal RAY sitting on the sofa with a pile of papers and folders laid out on the coffee table. He is studiously working his way through them and trying to concentrate. In frustration RAY throws his pen down onto the table. GETHIN enters a moment later through the glass doors. RAY spots him.

RAY   Back already? Thought you'd be ages yet. D'you have a good time?

GETHIN   It was alright.

RAY   Had a mate once who was always suspicious of anyone who said things were just 'alright'. Reckoned they had something to hide. (Beat) Park yourself there if you want to. I've just about had enough of this malarkey for tonight.

GETHIN   Problems?

RAY   Nothing a chat with the bank manager won't sort out. We've got a major deal going through, and trying to get the left leg to work with the right's like trying to push shit up hill with a tooth pick.

GETHIN   What is it? A big order?

RAY   Yeah. For the Olympics. There's going to be more
                merchandise than you can poke a stick at mate.
                Olympic watches, t-shirts, koalas. They're all cashing
                in. But ask yourself this, what do people really need
                at Olympics time, eh? Sunnies. Shades. Sunglasses.
                After all, they're going be sitting outside all day.
                Watching the runners, swimmers, and beach bloody
                volleyball. So I thought, "I'll have a bit of that", sent
                off the forms, crossed my fingers, and would you
                believe it? They gave me a licence to churn the
                bastards out and make a killing.

GETHIN   Great.

RAY   Christ yeah. I'm as happy as a dog with two dicks.
                Cost us three hundred thousand bucks mind, but
                we're going to be making these sunnies and shipping
                them out across Australia. Business up until then
                hadn't been too healthy. Well, to be honest, it was
                crook. So to make the dream work I had to talk to
                the bank. But that's alright, I know the business
                manager, Steve. Play golf together. Get on well so
                long as he's winning. But then the problems started.
                The designs for the sunnies had to go before a
                committee, and they weren't happy. So, I paid to get
                them redone, which cost a packet, overheads are
                rising, and I've got to go back to the bank and for

once in my life everything's going like a dream. I
finally get the design sorted out - the Olympic rings
stacked up on the frames like beer kegs - nice, yeah?
So we build the mouldings and start making the
bloody things.

GETHIN   So where's the problem?

RAY   Problem is the bloke running the machine wasn't
checking the frames when they came out of the press
every half hour like he was meant to. Well, to tell the
truth he was sitting out the back playing Tetrus.
When I get there in the morning I find we've got ten
thousand pairs of buggered frames, and I can't do a
thing with them.

GETHIN   Why not?

RAY   The dickhead put the moulding in the wrong way
round! The Olympic colours are running in the
wrong order! Instead of blue, yellow, black, green,
and red, they're going in reverse. Back to bloody
front!

GETHIN   Does it matter though? I mean, does it really matter
what colour they are as long as you've got five
Olympic rings?

RAY   Ah. That's another little blip. We haven't got five Olympic rings. We've got six. The moulding broke in the press.

GETHIN   You're kidding?

RAY   Well, more like five, and an oval shaped blob. *(Beat)* It's not easy being in business, mate. You try to do a good job, but the gods in government don't want a bar of it. All they want to know about is getting foreign companies in here quick. And when you start depending on other countries to help you out of the shit pile, you're asking for trouble, aren't you? They're saying Australia's a wealthy country, but I haven't seen any of it lately. So ask yourself this, where's all that money going? Not to me, my family, not to the ones who're doing the hard yards.

GETHIN   I suppose they're helping those who need it most.

RAY   Give everyone an equal chance. That's the only way of giving anyone a fair go. But no, they're spending a truckload on health care for Abos, and houses for Asians who can't even speak English yet. 'Course, you know what the main problem is. What all of this comes back to? *(Pause)* There's too many people in the country. I'm no racist mate, but if you've got a prime piece of land and for fifty years you've been getting a good crop from it, you don't suddenly decide to pull down the fence and walk away, do you? You don't turn your back and let the kangaroos in. Surely, the sooner the pollies realise that, the better?

GETHIN doesn't respond.

RAY   Yeah well, I don't suppose you want to about hear our problems, eh?

GETHIN   I'd better get to bed. I think they're planning a big day tomorrow.

RAY   Oh Gethin, before you go. I've been meaning to ask. Mee-gan. *(Beat)* You're not going to say anything, are you? Anything about Wales, that might upset her?

GETHIN   Me? 'Course not.

RAY   Good. Some things are best left buried, eh?

GETHIN   See you in the morning Ray.

RAY   Yeah. 'Night mate.

GETHIN slopes off stage-left. RAY sits for a moment, struggles with the work one last time, before giving in, shovelling up his papers and heading off left. RAY exits. Pause. RHODRI, CERI, and EMMA, appear and enter through the sliding glass doors. EMMA and CERI are singing drunkenly and performing the actions to the following song. RHODRI is trying to quieten them.

EMMA AND CERI   I want a home among the gum trees,
                      With lots of plum trees,
                      A sheep or two and a kangaroo.
                      A clothes line out the back,
                      Veranda at the front,
                      And an old, rocking chair.

RHODRI   Sshh! Sshh!

They giggle. RHODRI finally pushes the door open and they enter.

CERI   Yeah. We don't want to wake anyone up.

EMMA   Especially Gethin. Nobody is allowed to disturb Gethin.

CERI   That's the last thing you want.

EMMA   If anybody wakes the killjoy they die.

RHODRI   Sshh!

EMMA   Painfully.

*EMMA and RHODRI make their way to the sofa and collapse.
CERI falls into a chairs .*

CERI   It's oh so quiet...

EMMA   Sshh! Sshh!

RHODRI   You don't like the bloke much, do you?

CERI   Neither would you if you'd spent six months
              travelling across Australia with him.

EMMA   Gets on your tits after a while.

CERI   Like most of the men in your life, eh Em?

EMMA   Dream on Ceri boy.

RHODRI   Why'd he bother coming out here then?

EMMA   Good question. That's what I want to know.

CERI   It's either too hot, too expensive.

EMMA   Too much fun.

CERI   He peaked in Alice.

RHODRI   Why? What happened in Alice?

CERI   We were on a camping trip.

EMMA   Safari!

CERI   Ayre's Rock

EMMA   Uluru!

CERI   The Olgas, five days, and a canvas tent.

EMMA   "Safari so goody", remember?

CERI   Anyway, Gethin didn't want to go on this safari. So
               we said to him...

EMMA   "Stay at home you miserable bastard."

CERI   But he didn't.

EMMA   Unfortunately.

CERI   Gave in at the last minute.

EMMA   When he saw us filling our rucksacks and walking out the door. 'Didn't stop moaning the whole way up bloody Ayre's Rock.

CERI   Uluru!

EMMA   "Don't like camping. Can't sleep at night."

BOTH   "Don't feel safe."

EMMA   Pissed us off so much we moved out of the tent in the end.

CERI   Emma told the guide Gethin'd been making lewd suggestions to her during the night, so they swapped us with Mica and Herrard.

EMMA   Couple of German tourists trying to see the whole of Australia in seven days flat.

CERI   Thought they could drive across in a week.

EMMA   But that didn't stop him moaning about the food. Too salty. Too dry.

CERI   And shit, did he whinge about how dangerous it was. "What if we meet a dingo? What if we see a funnel web? What if I get bitten by a snake?"

EMMA   "Well why didn't you stay at the hostel then if you were so bloody worried? Piss off!"

CERI   The fact that the chances of being bitten were infinitesimal didn't come into it. The plain truth is that he loves complaining.

RHODRI   Mate of mine got bit once.

EMMA   Shit. What was it?

CERI   Taipan? Tiger snake?

RHODRI   Labrador.

EMMA   Ha!

RHODRI   Nah, nah. Took a great big chunk out of his leg. Jaws like a croc.

CERI   Yeah well, there were days with Gethin when you'd've happily thrown yourself on a Death Adder.

RHODRI   Sounds like a total woos.

CERI   He'll be a lot happier once he comes to terms with it.

RHODRI   What?

CERI   The big gee.

EMMA   His sexuality.

RHODRI You mean he's...

EMMA   Queer, yeah we do.

CERI   As a coot.

RHODRI He's a poofter?

CERI   Ha! Haven't heard that one since primary school.

CERI stretches out on the floor.

EMMA   How long d'you think we've known Cer?

CERI   Definitely? Since Rottnest.

EMMA   That's why he's moody all the time. 'Bats for the other side.

CERI   And she's not talking cricket.

RHODRI But he's never told you that he's, gay?

EMMA   That's the problem. He doesn't know yet.

RHODRI   So how can you be so sure then?

EMMA   I did go out with him for over a year, remember?

RHODRI   Yeah, but you're only guessing, aren't you?

EMMA   Erm, not really. The only time he's smiled during this entire holiday was on Rottnest. We were on the beach and Gethin's whingeing as per usual. "Don't like the seaside. Too hot. I'll burn." When all of a sudden he shuts up, and this grin, the biggest grin I've seen in my whole life, starts to grow on his face. 'Didn't think it was ever going to stop. Thought he was bad, didn't we Cer? Until I saw what he was looking at. Flesh. Men with biceps the size of grapefruit. Packets like Fyfe bananas. Couldn't drag him away that day. Or the next. Every morning without fail Gethin would plant himself in the sand and watch the muscle men running in and out of the water from the safety of his sun glasses. Transfixed.

CERI   Like a dog waiting for its dinner.

RHODRI   Have you asked him about it?

EMMA   Asked him? We've told him. "Gethin bach, you're gay. Face it and get on with your life for pity's sake."

RHODRI   What did he say to that?

EMMA   Stormed off in a huff. Thought we were winding him up.

RHODRI   Shouldn't you let him come out by himself, but?

EMMA   And put up with his miserable wep for the next five years? No fear. Whether he likes it or not, he's coming out. 'Sooner the better.

RHODRI   You can't jump to conclusions though.

EMMA   Rhodri. We caught him using talcum powder.

RHODRI   Shit.

EMMA   Exactly.

CERI has drifted off to sleep.

RHODRI   So you don't want to get back with him then?

EMMA   Well, that'd be a waste of time now wouldn't it? No, when Gethin decided, unilaterally, that our relationship should slow down to the point that it stalled, I should've guessed there was something else behind it all. *(Beat.)* Have you ever been stuck in a dud relationship, Rhodri?

RHODRI   No. Never gotten that far.

EMMA   But you've had girlfriends, haven't you?

RHODRI   Yeah. 'Course. Heaps.

EMMA   And how many's 'heaps'?

RHODRI   Erm, three.

EMMA   What went wrong?

RHODRI   Well, Melinda, the first one, said I didn't pay her enough attention or some shit. Thought I'd rather be in the pool than down the shops with her.

EMMA   It's a common complaint Rhodri. You should've gone out with another swimmer. That way it wouldn't have been an issue.

RHODRI   I did. Jody.

EMMA   And?

RHODRI   She ran off with the lifeguard.

EMMA   What about the third?

RHODRI   Rachel? Couldn't stick the smell of chlorine. Made her chuck.

EMMA   So there's hope then?

RHODRI   Hope?

EMMA leans forward and kisses RHODRI.

EMMA
A-ha. Hope.

They kiss again, and then break away momentarily. Pause. RHODRI laughs nervously.

EMMA   More?

RHODRI   Um. Yes. Please.

EMMA and RHODRI kiss, but more passionately this time. EMMA then peels off RHODRI's shirt. RHODRI breaks away.

RHODRI   Em. Not here. We can't do this here.

EMMA   Why not?

RHODRI   Ceri.

EMMA   He's sleeping.

RHODRI   What if he wakes up?

EMMA   He won't. He's a million miles away.

RHODRI   Yeah but...

EMMA gets up and kicks CERI. CERI doesn't flinch.

EMMA   Happy now?

RHODRI   Still...

EMMA   Are you saying you don't want to do this Rhodri?

RHODRI   No.

EMMA   Well, be quiet then.

They kiss. EMMA removes her top. RHODRI breaks off.

RHODRI   Emma. No. Mum chucks a mental when I get water
             on this lounge, God knows what she'd do if I...

EMMA   Alright, alright. Your room

EMMA pulls RHODRI centre stage. RHODRI laughs nervously.

EMMA   So we'll just have to go outside then, won't we?

RHODRI   Outside?

EMMA   Yeah. I've always wanted to do it in water.

RHODRI looks aghast. EMMA starts to undress until she is standing in only her underwear.

EMMA   What's the matter with you? You look like you're having a stroke.

RHODRI   You want to do it in the pool? The pool?

EMMA   It'll be exciting. How long d'you say you could hold your breath under water?

RHODRI   I didn't.

EMMA   Oh well, soon find out. It's times like this I'm glad I got my ten metres badge.

EMMA heads to the glass doors and steps outside onto the terrace.

RHODRI follows her to the door and stands open mouthed watching.
She goes off left and her bra is thrown back on to RHODRI. He runs
off after her. Pause. GWEN appears at the sliding glass doors at the
rear of the stage from the driveway, hears EMMA laughing and lokks
towards the pool. She enters the room and sees the scattered clothing on
the floor. She kicks it to one side and mutters something inaudible.
GWEN who has just returned from a night out clubbing, sits opposite
CERI and tips her loose change out onto the coffee table. The noise
disturbs CERI. He looks over at her and can't believe his eyes. He's a
little groggy.

CERI   Monique? Monique Stewart?

GWEN   Nah mate. Monique carked it.

CERI   Monique? Dead? No.

GWEN   Dropped off the back of a boat, remember? I used to
                be Monique. But now I'm Gwen. Gwen all the time.

CERI   Shit.

GWEN   Yeah, I was a bit upset about it too. Have a good
                night did you?

CERI   Yeah. Emma, Rhodri, me.

GWEN   Jeez. You persuaded my brother to go out to a night-club? What d'you do? Threaten to fill his paddling pool in?

CERI   Emma twisted his arm.

GWEN   I take it they're the ones rooting outside, are they?

CERI   Rooting?

GWEN   Like rabbits. You're trashed aren't you?

CERI   I'm sorry you died. I thought you were good.

GWEN   Thanks.

CERI   You're one of the main reasons I watch 'Shellcove Bay'. Or were. I think you're brilliant. Did you die brilliantly?

GWEN   It was pretty heart stopping.

CERI   I remember when you had your miscarriage. You were so, real.

GWEN   How much have you had?

CERI   And when Boris left you to join the priesthood. Ah, I was gutted.

GWEN   Too much by the look of it.

CERI   No, I'm not drunk. I research it you see. Television. I watch a lot of it. I'm starting a PhD when I go home.

GWEN   In telly?

CERI   Media Studies, yep.

GWEN   You study Australian soap operas? Jesus. What next?

CERI   'Want to know what my PhD title is?

GWEN   Reckon I'm going to hear it anyway.

CERI   "Australian Soap: Drama or Drug?"

GWEN   Nice.

CERI   You're my favourite. Along with Cindy. She's good too. But not better than you. You're on the same rung.

GWEN   You're not going to start stalking me, are you?

CERI   Michael the restaurant owner. Don't like him. He's a bastard.

GWEN   You're right there.

CERI   When he sacked you for turning up late I could've hit him, I could.

GWEN   Thanks.

CERI   I mean, if you'd over slept fair enough. Guilty as charged. But it's not your fault if you go into a bank and get taken hostage by a masked gunman now is it?

GWEN   Yeah, well. He's an alcoholic.

CERI   No? Has anyone told Georgie?

GWEN   Not on the show you dag. In real life.

CERI   Hey. I know what a dag is thank you very much.

GWEN   Could get through five hundred mil of vodka a day. Used to call him The Sponge.

CERI   Bit of dry shit hanging from a sheep's arse.

GWEN   And Melanie Robinson who works at the

newsagency? Well, she's just had her boobs done. Lifted.

CERI   I thought there was something different.

GWEN   And Tracy and Arnold? It's over.

CERI   No?

GWEN   It's all going to hit the fan in a couple of months. He's moving to Queensland.

CERI   They've had a hard life, haven't they? What with the car crash, cot death, house fire, attempted murder, abortion, kidnapping, HIV scare, and that younger woman on the motorbike. It's bound to put a strain on a marriage.

GWEN   You know a lot about this stuff don't you?

CERI   Like I said. I study it. I can tell you practically anything you want to know about 'Neighbours' since 1988. Want to know how many children Jim Robinson fathered? Exactly who's lived at number 32 Ramsay Street since the show started? Fire away. Feel free.

GWEN   I'll pass thanks.

CERI   I haven't just made a complete tit of myself have I?

GWEN   Yeah. But don't worry. I won't hold it against you.

GWEN stands.

GWEN   Don't suppose you want to come out tomorrow night? Friend of mine's having a thirtieth birthday party. It's going to be huge. You might even get to meet the rest of the Shellcove cast. I'm sure they'll be there.

CERI   Showbiz party, is it?

GWEN   Melanie's birthday. But if you ask me it's just a chance for her to show off her new assets, and thirty's a bit of a conservative estimate.

CERI   Lush.

GWEN   I thought you might say that.

CERI   Night Monique. I mean Gwen.

GWEN exits stage left. CERI smiles and follows her upstairs a little unsteadily a moment later. Pause. GETHIN enters. He sees the open glass door and looks out towards the swimming pool, smiles, and slides the door shut and locks it. He locks it, and heads back stage left. Turning out the lights as he leaves. Music. Blackout.

Act One - Scene Four

The following evening - Thursday. Lights rise to reveal RHODRI lying prostrate on the sofa. GWEN enters stage-left carrying a can of soft drink. She is smartly dressed and preparing to go out for the evening. She kicks RHODRI, he moves and she sits next to him and begins to apply the last of her make-up.

RHODRI   'Don't know how you manage it Gwen. Night after night.

GWEN   Stamina mate.

RHODRI   Don't you need twenty-four hours off to recover, but?

GWEN   Dunno. Never given it a go. Reckon I'd fall over and sleep for a week if I did. What's wrong with you anyway?

RHODRI   Tired.

GWEN   Wore you out did she? Don't think I've ever had sex in water. Unless standing under a shower with a construction worker called Tony counts.

RHODRI   What?

GWEN   Or maybe it was Terry.

RHODRI   You saw us?

GWEN   Couldn't miss you Rod. You weren't exactly being discreet.

RHODRI   You were watching us?

GWEN   Please! I might've caught a glimpse of your hairy arse going down into the water when I came home, but I most definitely wasn't perving.

RHODRI   Sounds like you were.

GWEN   Good on her. Hasn't been in Sydney more than three days and already she's getting down to business.

RHODRI   Took me by surprise.

GWEN   You've had a few work outs in that pool bruz, but never anything quite so exerting, eh? Shame it's not an Olympic event.

RHODRI   Don't be a dropkick, Gwen.

GWEN   At it all night were you?

RHODRI   Nah. Just couldn't get to sleep afterwards.

GWEN   The excitement?

RHODRI   The ute. Didn't realise it was so uncomfortable.

GWEN   How romantic. Why did you end up crashing out in the ute?

RHODRI   We had to! Someone'd locked the doors to the house by the time we were -

GWEN   Flaccid?

RHODRI   Finished.

GWEN   Don't look at me. I wasn't the last one upstairs, but I don't reckon Ceri would've locked you out.

RHODRI   Ceri knew about it?

GWEN   If you wanted privacy Rod you should've gone somewhere you could've drawn the curtains and pulled the door shut.

RHODRI   So who did then?

GWEN   Your guess is as good as mine. But if it was Mum or Dad they'd have spat long ago, I reckon. That only leaves thingy, doesn't it? The moody one. What's his name again?

RHODRI   Gethin.

GWEN   Is it? Oh. Well, must've been him. Wish Ceri'd get a move on. We'll have to leave soon.

RHODRI   Where's the party?

GWEN   Bondi. Should be a blast. Ceri's going to shit when he sees all those soap stars in one room.

EMMA enters, and joins RHODRI on the sofa.

GWEN   He's making a big effort to look good. After all, you've got to make a splash at these things haven't you? I'll leave you water babies to it.

GWEN exits stage-left.

RHODRI   Gwen reckons it was Gethin who locked us out.

EMMA   'Wouldn't surprise me. Sounds 'his style.

RHODRI   'Want me to get him to pull his head in?

EMMA   No. I'll deal with it.

GETHIN enters from the glass doors.

RHODRI   Speak of the devil.

GETHIN   Alright? I've had the best day. Been to Manly on the
             ferry. Great beach.

EMMA   Enjoyed yourself, did you?

GETHIN   Long. Clean. Hundreds of surfers.

EMMA   See anyone who caught your fancy?

GETHIN   Eh?

EMMA   You must be a sick bastard if you get a thrill playing
             these games with people, Gethin. Nobody thinks it's
             funny.

GETHIN   Sorry?

EMMA   Don't come the innocent. You know very well what I
             mean. It's childish.

GETHIN   What? What's this about?

EMMA   There's nothing wrong with it Gethin. Nobody'd mind. You're gay Gethin. Gay. Face it, and we'd all be a lot happier, including you.

GETHIN   I don't know what she's talking about.

EMMA   Yes you do. We all know. Just get it out your system, before you really fuck us off and you haven't got any friends left, alright?

GETHIN   I'm going.

EMMA   That's it. Run away. You can't go on like this Gethin. You can't.

GETHIN exits stage-left.

EMMA   Argh! He winds me up.

RHODRI   Forget about it.

EMMA   He'd be so much happier.

RHODRI   Leave him. Don't stress, hey?

GWEN and CERI enter stage left. CERI is smartly dressed all in black.

GWEN   Well, what d'you reckon?

RHODRI   Is that my top?

GWEN   Doesn't scrub up too badly does he?

RHODRI   And my pants?

GWEN   We had to borrow a few things.

RHODRI   He's wearing all my clothes.

GWEN   No he's not. He's got his own undies on.

RHODRI   Thank God.

GWEN   Yours didn't fit.

CERI   Do I look alright, Em?

EMMA   Phworr!

CERI   Not too much?

GWEN   When is it ever too much?

EMMA   Very sexy. You'll turn heads.

RHODRI   In my clothes.

GWEN   Which just goes to prove it's not what you wear but the way that you wear it. You ready?

CERI   Yep.

GWEN   Good. Let's find a taxi and eat. What's it to be? Thai, Vietnamese, Korean, Japanese, Greek, Indian?

CERI   Can't we get a burger?

GWEN   What d'you reckon?

RHODRI   Have fun.

GWEN   And you. But not too much, eh? You don't want to catch cold.

CERI and GWEN make an exit upstage centre.

RHODRI   D'you reckon there's something going on between those two?

EMMA   It wouldn't surprise me. He is gorgeous.

RHODRI   Reckon he's a spunk do you?

EMMA   God yeah. Eight-out-of-ten-girls who've expressed a preference wouldn't mind getting past first base with Ceri Llewelyn.

RHODRI   You never made it that far, but?

EMMA   Not officially. We got off together once.

RHODRI   What?

EMMA   We got off together. In our first year.

RHODRI   You pashed?

EMMA   If that's what I think it means, yeah, we did. He chatted me up at the bar and we got smashed beyond belief. 'Ended up in his room, and before I knew it we were sitting on his bed in nothing but our socks.

RHODRI   You slept with him?

EMMA   Well, not really. Technically we didn't sleep together. 'Didn't have sex.

RHODRI   Why not?

EMMA   Like I said, we'd had too much to drink. It was enough of an effort getting our kit off let alone attempt anything, hydraulic. After that we became good friends and, well, the pilot light just didn't spark.

RHODRI   Good. I didn't think you would've.

EMMA   Why?

RHODRI   I knew you wouldn't've done that.

EMMA   Getting all possessive are you?

RHODRI   No. No. You're just not, you're just not, like that are you?

EMMA   Like what?

RHODRI   Well. That. You wouldn't.

EMMA   Wouldn't what?

RHODRI   You know. You, you wouldn't do that with Ceri.

EMMA   <u>Why</u>?

RHODRI   Because, because, you're different.

EMMA   Different?

RHODRI   Yeah. 'Course you are.

EMMA   Huh. Different?

RHODRI   For sure.

EMMA   Different.

EMMA glares at RHODRI and after a pause hits him.

RHODRI   Hey!

EMMA starts to hit him with both hands. RHODRI tries to defend himself.

EMMA   Different! You bastard!

RHODRI   What?

EMMA   You fucking bastard!

RHODRI   Emma!

EMMA heads to the sliding doors.

EMMA   I should've known.

RHODRI   What?

EMMA exits.

RHODRI   Emma? Fucking hell. What's wrong?

RHODRI exits going after her. Pause. MEGAN enters stage-left. She walks over to the sliding doors and closes them. GETHIN enters from stage-left carrying an envelope.

MEGAN   Did you just hear something?

GETHIN   What?

MEGAN   Is everything alright between you and Emma?

GETHIN   Well, actually, we've broken up. Temporarily. When I told Emma I didn't want to move in with her last summer she threw a tantrum and things haven't been right since. 'Doesn't believe I'm committed to the relationship. Silly really. We're working through it though. *(Beat)* I brought the photos.

MEGAN   Ah right, well I haven't finished out front yet.

GETHIN   It won't take long. There aren't many.

GETHIN ploughs on regardless and rifles through the photographs.

GETHIN   This is the family photo Mum had taken last year. 'Made us go to a studio to have it done. 'Felt like a right pack of saddos, we did. Dad thinks we look wooden.

MEGAN   And what does your mother say to that?

GETHIN   Shoots him a look that could kill and tells him to be quiet. *(Beat)* Mum says that's you, her, and your best friend at school.

MEGAN   Mair.

GETHIN   Mari?

MEGAN   Mari Evans. 'Course. We used to call her Mari the mop because she never brushed her hair. 'Wonder what she's doing now?

GETHIN   She lives in Bridgend. Runs a hairdresser's. And this one's you and Mum in your St. David's Day outfits.

MEGAN   I'd forgotten the seld.

GETHIN   We couldn't keep everything when they sold the

house, but that's one thing Mum put by. And there's
Tadcu in the garden before he was ill.

MEGAN   Wonder where Ray is? I didn't think he'd be this
long.

GETHIN   Mum was saying just before we came out what a
shame it was you couldn't come back for the funeral.

MEGAN   It's so far, Gethin.

GETHIN   I know, I know. But still, Mum would've liked it.

MEGAN   I hope nothing's happened. That freeway can be
lethal. Hardly a week goes by now without some
kind of accident.

GETHIN   Oh, and another one of you.

MEGAN   Pardon?

GETHIN   You, Mum, and David. Lined up against his new car,
I think. Is that right? Mum went through one by one
and told me who all the unfamiliar faces were, filled
me in. Yeah, that's David. I was sorry to hear what
happened. It must have been difficult. I mean, it hit
you hard, I suppose. Hurt a lot, losing him like that.
I can't start to understand how you must've felt, but,

I'm sorry.

MEGAN   I didn't know there was a photograph.

GETHIN   After Tadcu died we had to sort through everything.

MEGAN   There was a photograph and nobody said.

GETHIN   Look Megan, Mum told me about the accident. I know what happened.

MEGAN   Why? What did she tell you?

GETHIN   The roads were wet. The car was going round a corner.

MEGAN   Is that what she said?

GETHIN   The tires slipped.

MEGAN   The same story.

GETHIN   You were devastated. Bound to be. After all, you were going to be married.

MEGAN   Still going 'round.

GETHIN   I know all about it, Megan. I know.

MEGAN   No Gethin. You don't.

GETHIN   I know what happened.

MEGAN   No. You just think you do.

GETHIN   Mum told me herself.

MEGAN   Everyone happy to make out it was a terrible accident. Awful accident. Mam, Dad, Ruth, happy pretending, when all the time they knew different.

GETHIN   Are you saying Mum's lied?

MEGAN   Just thinking about it now, makes me feel - oh God - makes me feel so... She still won't admit what really went on?

GETHIN   I don't understand. Didn't Mum tell me everything? Is that what you mean?

MEGAN   So cruel. I can feel the pain now. Like that day. The pain digging in -

GETHIN   Megan? 'Chi'n iawn?
               Are you alright?

MEGAN   Clean. Stinging. Oh God, I can feel it.

MEGAN exits stage-left.

GETHIN   Megan! What's this got... Megan! *(Beat. Under his breath.)* Fucking hell...

GETHIN places the photographs down on the table. Pause. He doesn't know what to do, but finally decides to follow MEGAN. Pause. RAY enters stage right carrying his briefcase and restlessly starts to look through a file. A moment later RHODRI surprises RAY when he enters through the sliding doors.

RAY   Rod? I thought you'd be out with the visitors.

RHODRI   Dad, have you seen Emma?

RAY   Is there something going on between you two I should know about, mate?

RHODRI   We were on the lounge.

RAY   Careful your mother doesn't catch you.

RHODRI   And all of a sudden she gets shitty with me, and runs out. Runs out into the street.

RAY   I thought she was going out with that other

character. Gethin.

RHODRI   Not anymore. He's gone gay.

RAY   Christ, you leave the house for the day and when you come home everything's upside down. Maybe your sister's seen her.

RHODRI   Nah, Gwen's out already.

RAY   And I suppose her mates'll be footing the bill?

RHODRI   Nah, it's Ceri tonight.

RAY   Ceri?

RHODRI   Yeah. All dressed up to some party. They were going together.

RAY   They're seeing each other?

RHODRI   Emma just went off on me. Like a bomb.

RAY   She's doing it to annoy me.

RHODRI   I don't know what happened y'know?

RAY   Stirring it up.

RHODRI   I've got to find out why she got snakey with me.

RAY   Yeah, right. Hang on Rod. I'll come with you.

RHODRI and RAY exit upstage centre. MEGAN enters stage left a moment later and goes over to the table. MEGAN picks up the photographs and silently starts to go through them until she finds one in particular. MEGAN stares at it. 'Soap Moment'. Blackout.

Act Two - Scene One

Lights rise. It is the next morning - Friday. GETHIN is standing by the stereo opening and closing the CD carriage; he is bored. EMMA enters from the sliding doors at the back of the stage. Music fades. They spot each other. GETHIN opens his mouth to say something but EMMA jumps in first.

EMMA   Look Gethin, before you start, I'm not in the mood, alright? The last thing I need right now are your smart remarks, digs, and bitchy comments. So do both of us a favour and just keep your gob shut, yeah?

GETHIN   Fine. He's very upset though.

EMMA   Didn't stand a chance, did I?

GETHIN   Nasty argument, was it?

EMMA   You could say that. We broke up.

GETHIN   Already? That's got to be some kind of world record, hasn't it? Even for you Emma.

EMMA   Didn't you hear a word I said? I don't want to talk about it.

GETHIN   Twenty-four hours. Less than twenty-four hours.

EMMA   Point taken. Now will you please leave it be? We don't want blood on the carpets.

GETHIN   I'm surprised that's all.

EMMA   You're surprised?

GETHIN   Pissed you off, did he?

EMMA   Gethin. It was a serious lapse of judgement and it's over.

GETHIN   So why d'you run off?

EMMA   I didn't run off. I went for a walk.

GETHIN   By yourself?

EMMA   Yes, because I didn't want to be left alone in the same house as that pig. You don't think people like that exist, do you? Well you know they do, hear about it all the time, but you don't expect the person you're shagging to open their mouth and come out with crap like that.

GETHIN   So, you shagged him then?

EMMA　　　There's no winning with you, is there?

GETHIN　　Tell me what happened.

EMMA　　　Promise you won't say anything?

GETHIN　　Cross my heart.

EMMA　　　No, serious Geth. Ceri'd go ape-shit if he found out what's been said. You can't go spreading this round like you normally would, alright?

GETHIN　　Sounds juicy. What's it got to do with Ceri?

EMMA　　　I still can't believe it.

GETHIN　　What? Tell me before I die of suspense, will you?

EMMA　　　Last night I was sitting here with Rhodri, yeah? Just the two of us.

GETHIN　　I saw, remember? Talk about teenagers at the back of the bus.

EMMA　　　D'you do it deliberately, or what?

GETHIN　　You were!

EMMA   And he asks me whether or not I think Ceri's sexy. I say, "Hello! 'Course he is." You'd have to be blind not to want to wake up beside that in the morning, right?

GETHIN   Yeah. I mean... Would you?

EMMA   So I'm telling him all about the time Ceri and me had our little fling.

GETHIN   Ceri and you had a fling?

EMMA   A-ha.

GETHIN   You never told me.

EMMA   Didn't I? Oh, well. We did.

GETHIN   A fling?

EMMA   Calm down Gethin. It was before we got together.

GETHIN   How long for?

EMMA   Well, I wouldn't even call it a fling actually. More a one night stand.

GETHIN   I don't believe this. You flung?

EMMA   Nothing happened. We just took our clothes off and giggled.

GETHIN   Giggled? What's that? Some kind of kinky game we never got round to trying?

EMMA   I know you find it hard to believe but there was a time when we weren't going out together, y'know? A time when I was happy. Pre-you. Just the same as now. Post-you. Post-Gethin. Look, d'you want to know what happened last night, or not?

GETHIN   'Course I do. Just don't go giving me a heart attack with any more revelations about your sexual conquests and my best friends.

EMMA   Ttt. So I tell Rhodri about that one night with Ceri, and he knows we didn't, y'know, do anything. Says he knew deep down I would never have done that with Ceri. Just knew it.

GETHIN   Why?

EMMA   Hang about. I'm coming to that. Because we're "different".

GETHIN   Different? What does that mean?

EMMA   Oh, come on Gethin, catch up bach. "Different."
                I'm white. Ceri's black.

GETHIN   Bloody hell.

EMMA   I thought he was pissing about. He's looking me
                straight in the eye and these words I can't for the life
                of me believe are coming out his mouth.

GETHIN   What did you do?

EMMA   What any other decent person would've done.
                Thumped him.

GETHIN   Christ. Are you sure?

EMMA   'Course I am. I sprained my wrist in the process.
                Now you can see the difficult position I'm in. I don't
                want to cause a scene Gethin, but I can't stick
                around here and make polite conversation over
                dinner knowing Rhodri thinks that way about Ceri,
                now can I? And to make matters worse Ceri's
                decided to make a move on Gwen.

GETHIN   He's never?

EMMA   Shit.

GETHIN   No?

EMMA   Shit Emma. You weren't supposed to say anything.

GETHIN   Gwen? He's trying it on with Gwen?

EMMA   Gethin, don't say anything. Please? It was meant to
              be private.

GETHIN   Ceri and Gwen?

EMMA   It was just something he mentioned. Something he
              fancied trying.

GETHIN   What? Like climbing the Harbour Bridge?

EMMA   I can't believe I told you. It was the one thing I had
              to remember not to do.

GETHIN   Cheers.

EMMA   You know what I mean. If anyone tells you a secret
              they might as well cut out the middle man and take
              out a full page ad in The Western Mail. Not a word
              Gethin, eh? Not to Rhodri, Ray, or Megan.

GETHIN   You don't want to worry about Megan. She's got her own fish to fry.

EMMA   Why Gethin? What've you done now?

GETHIN   Last night. I gave her the photos.

EMMA   You didn't cause a scene, did you?

GETHIN   No. 'Course not

EMMA   Good.

GETHIN   She just got a little bit upset.

EMMA   You're dangerous, you are.

GETHIN   I had to say something. I did! But then she started going on about how I don't know the full story, and how Mum still won't admit the truth.

EMMA   Oh, Gethin.

GETHIN   And I'm completely awake by now, I mean, my ears are flapping, and I start thinking, "Hang about, why's she bringing Mum into it?" There's something funny going on here Emma, and I intend to get to the bottom of it.

EMMA   Oh God, he thinks he's Inspector Morse.

GETHIN   She's never once gone home, and it isn't as though she couldn't afford the airfare.

EMMA   Or should that be Miss. Marple?

GETHIN   I'm telling you, there's more to her than meets the eye.

EMMA   And you should leave well alone. After all, what was that good piece of advice your mother gave you before we left?

GETHIN   "Go easy. Be sensitive." But...

EMMA   No buts. She didn't want you to upset Megan, did she?

GETHIN   No.

EMMA   So don't. If you want to get the full story, pester your mother when you get back, but for the time being, leave Megan be. After all, we're guests in her house Gethin, and harrassing the poor woman over something that happened years ago, just wouldn't be polite, now would it?

GETHIN   What're you going to do about Rhodri?

EMMA   Hope he doesn't breathe on me let alone talk to me, because if he does, I'm not going to hold my tongue. And not a word about Gwen and Ceri to anyone, right? We'll be off in a few days and with any luck we can get out of this place without causing a scene. Jesus. Why do all the men in my life turn out to be such twats?

EMMA exits stage-left leaving GETHIN to ponder her final statement. Almost immediately RHODRI enters up centre.

RHODRI   Geth? Is she back?

GETHIN   You'd better leave her Rod. She's not a happy bunny.

RHODRI   Did she say why she spun out like that?

GETHIN   No.

RHODRI   Nothing?

GETHIN   What exactly happened between you two last night?

RHODRI   We were sitting on the sofa having a yabber, y'know?

If I've stuffed up I wish she'd say something.

GETHIN   What were you talking about?

RHODRI   Nothing major. She was just telling me about the time she and Ceri nearly did the business, but didn't. Ceri couldn't get a bar up, y'know?

GETHIN   Really? Oh, really?

RHODRI   I know Emma's different…

GETHIN   Different?

RHODRI   Yeah. I've never been with anyone like her before. She's different. Special. So I tell her that, she gets dark on me, and I cop the serve of my life. Are you sure she didn't say anything, mate?

GETHIN   Nothing springs to mind. She's just really really really pissed off with you. Try not to let it get to you down, eh?

GWEN enters stage-left - she has just woken up. She goes to the fridge to get some water.

GWEN   Don't talk to me. Don't come near me. My head is about to implode.

RHODRI   Jeez Gwen, you've got a face like a robber's dog on you this morning. What d'you get up to last night?

GWEN   What didn't I? White powder up there, a pill or two in here, and plenty of champers to wash it all down.

GETHIN   You seen Ceri this morning?

GWEN   Hey? Who? Oh, it's you. Graham.

GETHIN   Gethin.

GWEN   Whatever. No, not since I fell out of a taxi at five o'clock and he picked me up off the pavement. Must be still in bed.

RHODRI   Oh yeah?

GWEN   Jeez you're a dag Rod.

MEGAN enters stage-left. She is in a terrible temper.

MEGAN   Rhodri, have you moved that ute from the front of the house yet, say?

RHODRI   I've been busy Mum.

MEGAN   Get it off the drive and into the garage. I don't want to see that rattletrap every time I look out the window.

RHODRI   But.

MEGAN   Now!

RHODRI turns and goes outside.

MEGAN   And look at the state on you Gwen. What in hell's name have you been doing to yourself?

GWEN   I know, I know. I look like shit, smell like it too, and the shower's empty.

MEGAN   Good, and you can come straight back afterwards to give me a hand. I don't see why I should be the only person in this house who lifts a finger. Alright?

GWEN   Fabulous.

GWEN exits stage-left.

GETHIN   O's 'na unrhwybeth alla i 'neud i helpu?
               Is there anything I can do to help, Megan?

MEGAN   No thanks Gethin. Just go outside and enjoy the sunshine, eh?

GETHIN waits for MEGAN to say something else. She doesn't. Pause. GETHIN exits up centre. MEGAN wipes down the breakfast bar. RAY enters stage-left.

RAY   Seen my tie love?

MEGAN   Why does everyone in this house assume I know where everything is and expect me to be able to lay my hand on it at a second's notice?

MEGAN exits up centre.

RAY   Maybe it's because you're the one that tidies everything up.

RAY searches for the tie. CERI enters stage-left - he has just woken up.

CERI   Morning.

RAY   Oh, morning Ceri mate. You look like you had a good time last night.

CERI   That bad, eh?

RAY   I wouldn't've expected anything less. I've heard

Gwen come home at six in the morning enough times to know she likes a big night out.

CERI   She knew everyone there. That's what amazed me. Mind you it was a 'Shellcove Bay' party.

RAY   And what did you make of that mob?

CERI   Well, I never thought when I came to Australia I'd be mixing in those circles. Champagne on tap, paparazzi on the doorstep. It was mad.

RAY   Yeah, seems like a good life that TV caper, doesn't it? But it's hard y'know? The number of times Gwen's phoned us up in a state 'cause of the pressure she was under...

CERI   Really?

RAY   Don't get me wrong. Gwen loved working on Shellcove. That's why she took it so badly when they put her off. Didn't want to eat, didn't talk to anyone, didn't want to go out partying with her mates, and that's when you can tell there's something seriously wrong with Gwen, eh?

CERI   I didn't realise.

RAY   She was in a state for months, but now she's back on her feet and looking brighter. It didn't help that she'd just broken up with her boyfriend. That was another knock Gwen didn't need. Mee-gan's taken time to see her right, but we're still protective. Even now. Don't want her getting any set backs, y'know?

CERI   'Course not.

RAY   So you'd tell us, wouldn't you, if there was anything going on? I know she has her boyfriends, but we like to know exactly what the score is see, just in case something does happen Ceri, and well, Gwen needs us.

CERI   Sure.

RAY   So? Is there anything between you and Gwen that Mee-gan and me should know about? I just ask you to be honest with me Ceri. That's all.

CERI   No. We're just mates.

RAY   Mates?

CERI   Yeah. Gwen's showing me 'round.

RAY   Good. I mean, it's good to know these things so we can keep an eye out for her y'know?

GWEN enters stage-left.

RAY   Ceri was just telling me about your night on the town, love. Sounds like you had a ball.

GWEN   It was alright.

RAY   Alright, she says! And you had enough cash for the taxi home and everything? 'Cause you've only got to ask Gwen, if you're short.

GWEN   You feeling alright, Ray?

RAY   Yeah, why shouldn't I? Anyway, better go. Got a meeting with the bank at eleven, and the rat with the gold tooth doesn't like it if you turn up late. See you later.

RAY exits stage-right.

CERI   Yeah. Bye.

GWEN   Jeez, wonder what came over him. He's never offered me money before. Must be going senile.

GWEN kisses CERI.

GWEN   Mmmm. So, what would you call that then Welsh boy?

CERI   That? That just now? Erm, six out-of-ten?

GWEN punches him playfully.

CERI   Oh, right, that'd be a...

CERI kisses GWEN.

CERI   Cusan. Why? What would you Aussies call it?

GWEN   A toungie. It might not have the same poetry but...

CERI   It means the same thing.

They kiss again.

GWEN   You were getting very friendly with Melanie last night. 'Couldn't take your eyes off her fun bags.

CERI   Were you spying on me?

GWEN   I know what those girls are like. Given ten minutes and the opportunity they'd've stolen you away for a quick root.

CERI   And how would you know?

GWEN   I've been there, remember?

CERI   You've stolen other women's boyfriends?

GWEN   Boyfriends, husbands, fathers, sons.

CERI   Sounds like you've played the field.

GWEN   No. Never been with a footballer. Not yet anyway.

CERI   Should I be worried then?

GWEN   Nah, you're O.K. You're different.

GWEN and CERI kiss. GETHIN enters and spots them. Pause.
GETHIN turns and exits unnoticed. Blackout.

Act Two - Scene Two

The next day - Saturday. CERI and EMMA are sitting around the breakfast bar. CERI is counting money.

EMMA Well I don't understand where it's gone. I've hardly spent a cent since we got here.

CERI So who was it spent a hundred and fifty dollars on a dress in Melbourne, then?

EMMA I meant since we arrived in Sydney. Besides, it was reduced and even you said it looked fabulous.

CERI Face facts Emma, we've got less than fifty dollars between us and four full days left in Australia. We're going to have a blast, aren't we?

EMMA What about the credit card? Is that full?

CERI Might as well cut it up for all the good it'll do us.

EMMA We can't live off fifty dollars Ceri. We'll have to ask Gethin for a loan. I know he's got plenty of cash in that grubby money belt of his.

CERI Doesn't buy anything, do anything...

EMMA   Or know how to enjoy himself.

CERI   We'd all be rich if we lived like that.

EMMA   But then again. I'm the last person he's going to lend money to, aren't I?

CERI   Lucky we made it this far without killing him. At least we've got a roof over our heads.

EMMA   You can talk. You've done brilliantly out of this arrangement.

CERI   What?

EMMA   All your fantasies come real.

CERI   Don't know what you mean, Emma.

EMMA   You've been dreaming about getting inside that woman's knickers from day one. Praying you'd get a chance to work the soap queen into a lather.

CERI   Alright, alright. You've made your point.

EMMA   Dirty boy.

CERI   Jealous cow.

EMMA   Eighteen women in six-months. I'm surprised it's
            still in one piece. Seven Aussies, six Brits, two
            Americans, one Japanese, an Italian...

CERI   Youth hostels. The ultimate knocking shop.

EMMA   And that Spaniard you took advantage of in Saint
            Kilda. Talk about the United Nations.

CERI   Hey, I didn't take advantage of anyone Spanish in
            Saint Kilda. She was Portuguese.

EMMA   Small detail.

CERI   I still say you didn't give Rhodri long enough.

EMMA   Trust me Ceri. It was a dead end.

CERI   So? You could've strung him along a bit. Had your
            fun, then given him the flick.

EMMA   Or flown home with a promise that I'd e-mail him
            every day?

CERI   Gwen knows we can't start anything serious.

EMMA   Not with fifty dollars to your name you can't.

CERI   Forty-three sixty to be exact.

EMMA   We could try Ray. He's always going on about how much money he's got.

CERI   You could, but I can't see him lending me five cents let alone five dollars.

EMMA   I've warned you about slagging off the Aussie football team. Someone's going to thump you one of these days if you don't look out.

CERI   He knows something's up between me and Gwen.

EMMA   What makes you say that?

CERI   He asked if Gwen was going out with anyone.

EMMA   Serious? What d'you say?

CERI   Nothing of course. It's none of his bloody business who I'm seeing, and I know Gwen's had enough of him sticking his nose into her love-life.

EMMA   Good for you.

CERI   Wonder how he got on to us though. It's not like we

were flaunting it outside in the swimming pool now
was it?

EMMA   I wasn't flaunting nothing.

CERI   So, how did he find out?

EMMA   I've got a fair idea.

CERI   Nah. You don't think he's at it again, do you?

EMMA   Mighty mouth? Who else?

CERI   But how does Gethin know?

EMMA   Erm, would now be a good time to confess?

CERI   Suddenly it all makes sense.

EMMA   It slipped out.

CERI   And he's gone off and started yapping. It was meant
to be a secret Emma, a secret...

EMMA   I told him not to say anything. Begged him Ceri.

CERI   Doesn't work with Gethin.

EMMA He can't keep doing this. He's got to learn. He can't keep doing this. He has to be told. I've had a fucking 'nough of it. I'm not going back to Wales with him lying and moaning like there's no tomorrow. *(She moves to the sliding doors)* Gethin! Gethin!

CERI Here we go. Emma? What're you going to say to him?

EMMA The truth. And this time he's going to listen. Gethin!

CERI Go easy. We still need a place to stay, remember?

EMMA It's for the best Ceri. It's time to finish it.

GETHIN enters up centre.

GETHIN D'you want something?

EMMA You really can be a little shit when you want to be.

GETHIN What have I done now?

EMMA I asked you not to say anything, but you went straight out and told the world.

GETHIN What're you talking about Emma?

EMMA   Ceri and Gwen. You had to open your gob, didn't
            you?

GETHIN   No. I haven't told anyone about Ceri and Gwen's
            little affair.

EMMA   Bollocks Gethin. Bollocks. We know you told Ray.

GETHIN   I didn't tell a soul!

EMMA   Well he knows, and I didn't say a word, neither did
            Ceri, so who else could it have been?

CERI   The evidence is pretty strong.

EMMA   You've been stirring up trouble at every opportunity,
            Gethin. Why break the habit of a lifetime?

GETHIN   I did not tell Ray about Ceri and Gwen. I know what
            Ray's like.

EMMA   That's why you did it. You knew he'd get involved.

GETHIN   Emma, listen to me. I did not spill a single word.
            Jesus, what's your problem? You've been like this
            ever since you failed your degree.

EMMA   You're the one with the problem. We've been telling you that for months now.

GETHIN Again? Aren't you tired of this yet?

EMMA Gethin. You're gay. Gay. Gay. Gay. Gay. Gay.

GETHIN Like that word, don't you?

EMMA We don't mind if you're attracted to men. Makes no difference to us, does it Ceri?

CERI No, none at all.

EMMA We don't mind having a gay friend. We just don't want a moody evil one, that's all. So why don't you just go out there and get on with it, eh? For everyone's sake.

GETHIN For your sake, you mean?

EMMA Yes, my sake. I'm tired of it Gethin. It's not funny anymore. Face facts and get on with it, else...

GETHIN Else what? What're you going to do?

EMMA What you seem to do so brilliantly. Tell everyone. Nice bit of gossip that, eh Ceri? Should set tongues wagging for weeks.

GETHIN   You wouldn't?

EMMA   I asked you not to say anything. Was it really that hard?

GETHIN   I didn't tell Ray.

EMMA   Don't believe you.

GETHIN   Ceri?

CERI   Sorry mate.

GETHIN   So what d'you want me to do? Go gay? Find a man? Try it? Is that what you're really suggesting?

EMMA   Honestly? Yes. That's what I want. I want you to go out there, meet a man, take all your clothes off, fuck him senseless, and get on with life. Maybe then, you'll get all this mean, poisonous business out of your system. Maybe then, I might start to like you again. But as things stand Gethin, I don't want to know you, I don't want to see you, or be in the same room as you. I don't want to know someone who's so fucked up inside that it's showing itself in the cruel tricks he plays on people he calls his friends. I want you to sort yourself out. I want you to smile again. I want you to be happy for fuck's sake.

GETHIN looks around dazed at his friends and then moves to the sliding doors.

CERI   Gethin? Gethin?

GETHIN exits.

CERI   Gethin mun! Come here! You didn't have to be so hard on him Emma.

EMMA   No? Then why did he cool things down between us, Ceri? Why?

EMMA exits slowly stage left, and CERI watches her go.

CERI   Emma. Emma, look... You don't know, alright? You don't... Em!

CERI tries to decide who to follow. He chooses GETHIN and leaves through the glass doors. Pause. RAY enters stage-right in a foul mood. He throws his papers down and gets a drink from the fridge. MEGAN enters through the patio doors carrying a shopping bag.

MEGAN   Where are the boys off to?

RAY   Eh?

MEGAN   Ceri and Gethin. Heading up the road.

RAY   No good asking me. I've just got back.

MEGAN produces a newspaper from the shopping bag and gives it to RAY.

MEGAN   Funeral of that boy was held today. The lad who died on the freeway.

RAY   The Lebanese?

MEGAN   Front page. Turns out he was Korean. Somebody Yim. Seems we were all wrong about what happened, eh? Looks like he'd been under a lot of pressure at school and his girlfriend had just broken it off with him. Couldn't cope. He went up to the overpass and climbed onto the railings. Fifteen years old. There's no hope, is there?

MEGAN exits and RAY flicks through the paper. Something catches his attention. He stands. RAY reads the paper again before looking around the house for MEGAN.

RAY   Mee-gan! Mee-gan!

MEGAN enters.

MEGAN   What can't you find now?

RAY   Have you seen it?

MEGAN   What?

RAY   The photo. Have you seen the photo?

MEGAN   What photo?

RAY   The one in the paper. The one of your daughter and that boy, that boy who told me there was nothing going on, glued together at the lips. This photo!

MEGAN takes the newspaper.

RAY   You take them into your house, you ask them a straightforward no bull shit question and this is how they repay you. With lies.

MEGAN   Ray.

RAY   He sat there Mee-gan, and swore there was nothing going on. Look at them. All over each other. I'm surprised they've still got their clothes on the rate they're going at it.

MEGAN   Don't get worked up Ray.

RAY   Read it! Read what it says.

RAY snatches the newspaper back from MEGAN.

MEGAN   Ray.

RAY   "Gwen Seghuh, former star of 'Shellcove Bay', stepped out last night with handsome new boyfriend Ceri Llewelyn, a young academic from the UK. Gwen wasn't talking to reporters at the glam party to celebrate co-star Melanie Robertson's thirtieth birthday, but the smile on her face said it all." *(Beat)* Gwen's done this on purpose Mee-gan. She knew what I'd say after the last fiasco.

MEGAN   Calm down.

RAY   My daughter's splashed all over the papers with her tongue down the throat of a man she hardly knows and you expect me to calm down? That really takes the cake, that does. She doesn't know him from Adam! She keeps taking these risks. How can she be sure she's going to be safe, eh? After last time, how does she know?

MEGAN   Ray!

RAY   She makes jokes at my expense. Hasn't got a pinch of respect for me. Nothing. So she can just get out of here if that's how she wants it, because I'm not standing for it anymore Mee-gan. Not again.

GWEN and CERI enter laughing from outside through the sliding doors.

MEGAN   Gwen?

RAY   You lied to me.

GWEN   About what?

RAY   I asked him if you were going out together and he said you were just mates.

CERI   We are.

RAY   Don't try it on matey. I know different.

MEGAN gives GWEN the newspaper.

MEGAN   Look love, why don't we leave it be and take...

RAY   Well? What've you got to say for yourself?

GWEN   They haven't got my best side granted, but you
            don't want...

RAY   This is not a joke Gwen. Everything is not a joke. He
            lied to me and I want an explanation.

CERI   Come on Ray, you didn't really expect me to tell you
            the truth, did you? After all, It's none of your
            business, is it?

RAY   None of my business? She's my child.

GWEN   Ray! I'm twenty-nine!

RAY   So, why don't you act it then?

EMMA enters stage left.

RAY   She's my daughter. Don't you think I have a right to
            know who she's going out with?

CERI   Frankly? No.

RHODRI enters up centre.

RAY   I want you out of this house. I want your things
            packed and I want you out.

GWEN   Fair go, Ray.

RAY   You are no longer welcome. Understand?

CERI   Christ Ray. It's not the end of the world, y'know?

RAY   It isn't, is it?

CERI   No. Who your daughter chooses to have sex with has nothing to do with you. And being her father, I'm surprised, to be perfectly truthful, to find you taking such an interest in the matter.

RAY   What did you just say?

CERI   Come on. It's a bit strange isn't it really? How old are you?

RAY   Are you trying to be clever?

CERI   Clever? No. Honest? Yes.

GWEN   Ceri. Leave it.

RAY   You're doing this on purpose.

RHODRI   Dad. Don't.

RAY   Reckon you're smarter than me, don't you? With your qualifications and big degree?

CERI   PhD actually. But yeah.

RAY goes to punch him. They struggle.

MEGAN   Ray!

GWEN   No! Get off him! Get off!

GWEN is trying to separate the men.

GWEN   Dad! No! Stop it. It's not his fault. How d'you reckon that picture got in the papers, eh? Because of me. Because I wanted it. I wanted my face in the weeklies. You're nobody unless you get seen Dad. You know that. *(Beat)* I took Ceri out. I showed him off. Big, handsome black man. Bound to make a splash. Bound to, yeah Dad? So, I made sure everyone saw him and when I knew the cameras were looking our way, I kissed him. Bang. Photo in the paper. Gwen's in the paper. Gwen's in the news. And how long's it been since you could say that Dad? Months? Don't you miss it? Don't you miss the buzz you get hearing people talk about me? I do. I miss it. I miss it so badly. He's nothing Dad. Just a photo. Please. Believe it.

RAY looks at GWEN in shock. Pause. RAY releases CERI, turns and exits hurriedly up centre. GWEN looks at CERI, he looks away.

MEGAN   Ray! Ray!

MEGAN follows Ray up centre but does not leave. Silence. In shock GWEN moves to leave stage left. EMMA obstructs her on the stairs.

EMMA   Bitch.

GWEN ignores the comment and continues moving, but EMMA grabs hold of her.

EMMA   How dare you!

GWEN   You don't understand.

EMMA   Yes I do. And like I said before. Bitch.

MEGAN   Emma. Let her go. Emma.

GWEN exits.

EMMA   I should've known you'd stick up for her.

MEGAN   Emma. Let it rest.

EMMA   Aren't you going to say something?

MEGAN   Not now.

RHODRI   Emma, it's over.

EMMA   I suppose that's how everything works with you people, isn't it? You'll let her run off. You won't make her deal with it.

RHODRI   Cool down, hey?

EMMA   Gethin was right. That's what you did, wasn't it? You ran away.

MEGAN   Please Emma. Settle.

EMMA   You couldn't cope with David dying.

MEGAN   How do you know about that?

RHODRI   Mum?

EMMA   Fine, keep running. Let everyone around you run too. But it's not right, Megan.

MEGAN   This has got nothing to do with you.

RHODRI Who's David?

EMMA No, thank God. Because I'll be leaving soon. I'll be out of this messed up family.

RHODRI Will somebody tell me what's going on?

EMMA You've got a husband, who judging by tonight's little performance is standing on the brink of a nervous breakdown, a daughter who's hiding away behind drugs and drink because she won't face the truth, and a son who's so, so, so stupid he actually believes the arguments of brain dead politicians who say white is better than black. And you say you're not pretending? You've got to be kidding, woman. Open your eyes, will you?

EMMA looks at Ceri, he looks away. 'Soap Moment'. Blackout.

Act Two - Scene Three

Very early the next morning - Sunday. It is dark outside. MEGAN is alone on stage. She is in the living room threading the tape out from the audio cassette she brought in during the first act. RAY appears behind the sliding doors. He waits for a moment before deciding to come in. Silence.

MEGAN   Gethin was telling me about one of the boys in his class. New to the area and starting school. But there was one thing Gethin couldn't understand. He wouldn't stop talking however much Gethin told him to be quiet. "Bydd dawel," he'd say. "Jason, bydd dawel." But Jason didn't take any notice. Didn't seem to hear a single word. So Gethin went over, knelt down and asked, "Jason? What's tawel?" And Jason looked at Gethin as if he was mad. "Thing you wipe your face with." Poor kid was English. I asked and asked Ray.

RAY   Sorry.

MEGAN   Not good enough. You knew how important it was for me to show Gethin and his friends a nice time while they were here. I've been looking forward for months. Did you have to blow up like that? Did you have to go spoil it? *(Beat)* All Gethin could do was laugh. A classroom full of kiddies and their teacher

384

laughing like a drain.

RAY   Has everyone gone to bed?

MEGAN   Hours ago. Don't think they could face me. Did you do it on purpose?

RAY   No.

MEGAN   To spite me?

RAY   'Course not.

MEGAN   The only people from home to visit in thirty years and you behave like that. God knows what they must think now.

RAY   She'll be right.

MEGAN   You don't know. You don't know that. You can't afford to lose your temper, Ray. What would a client say if you went off like that in a meeting, eh? What then?

RAY   Mee-gan.

MEGAN   You've got to keep a cool head for the sake of the business if nothing else.

RAY   You don't have to worry about the business.

MEGAN   Oh no. I'd forgotten. That's your responsibility, isn't it? For God's sake, Ray.

RAY   It's over. Finished.

MEGAN   Don't change the subject. Don't -

RAY   The bank won't loan us another cent.

MEGAN   I'm serious Ray.

RAY   They've stopped financing us. Recalled what we owe. They didn't approve the application, Mee-gan.

MEGAN   You said they had.

RAY   To stop you going on. I couldn't stand the questions.

MEGAN   No Ray. You're wrong. Talk to Steve. Get him to sort it out.

RAY   Steve's not there, Mee-gan. He's been suspended. Too many favours. Too many quick decisions on big loans with no collateral. They reviewed the files. Saw how much money he's been loaning the firm. They won't give us any more. I haven't paid wages for a fortnight. Suppliers are refusing credit. I can't cover the phone bill. Look love, if the climate was different. If Canberra was backing business instead of strangling us with both hands we'd be right. We might stand a chance.

MEGAN   No Ray. Don't.

RAY   But when they're more interested in helping migrants who've only been in the country five-minutes, what chance have we got?

MEGAN   Stop it! Stop it Ray!

RAY   Give everyone a fair go, eh?

MEGAN   Over and over.

RAY   Mee-gan -

MEGAN   No! I don't want to hear another word. I've heard enough excuses. We can't carry on lying. For years we've told Rhodri he can be a champion swimmer. He's twenty-two Ray. There are sixteen year-olds swimming faster than he ever will.

RAY   He's good though.

MEGAN   He practices in a pool in the back garden! When was
           the last time he trained at the institute? We've lied
           Ray and it's not fair. Since Gwen left the show she
           hasn't known whether she's coming or going, but
           we've fed her dream she'll get a second chance.
           We've led them both on when we shouldn't've. But
           we're not going to do that now. Not anymore. We
           can't lie about this.

RAY   Mee-gan.

MEGAN   We have to face the truth. We can't carry on acting
           like it isn't a problem Ray. We've got to sort it out.
           Ourselves. No more pretending. Let's stop
           pretending. Please?

RAY   I'm tired Mee-gan.

MEGAN   I know.

RAY   'Don't know if I've got the energy to go on.

MEGAN hugs RAY. He wilts.

RAY   Fifteen Mee-gan. That boy was fifteen.

MEGAN   I know. It's late. Go to bed, eh? It's late.

RAY exits stage-left. MEGAN takes a moment to herself before preparing the house for the night. GETHIN appears behind the sliding doors. He presses his face up against the glass, looking in for signs of life, and spots MEGAN. There is a moment of embarrassment when their eyes meet. GETHIN comes in.

MEGAN   Gethin? Everything alright?

GETHIN   Fine. Why?

MEGAN   You seem surprised to see me.

GETHIN   Do I?

MEGAN   Yes.

GETHIN   Thought you'd be in bed by now.

MEGAN   I'm on the way. How was your night?

GETHIN   Alright.

MEGAN   You found Oxford Street, then?

GETHIN   Who said I was going there?

MEGAN   Ceri. He was worried.

GETHIN   Don't know why. I just went to see what it was like.
              Out of interest.

MEGAN   It must have been very interesting for you to stay out
              'til now. It's two o'clock.

GETHIN   There was no need for Ceri to be worried.

MEGAN   I think it was because you were by yourself.

GETHIN   I wasn't.

MEGAN   No?

GETHIN   No. I'm not completely anti-social, y'know?

MEGAN   Didn't say you were Gethin.

GETHIN   Emma thinks I am, but I can make friends when I
              want to.

MEGAN   So? What was his name?

GETHIN   Tt. Nick. We talked, played pool, drank a few
              schooners, had a laugh, came home.

MEGAN   Sounds like you're giving evidence.

GETHIN   Does it?

MEGAN   You don't have to look so frightened Gethin. I'm not going to tell you off.

GETHIN   Thank you.

MEGAN   Doesn't matter to me that you're gay.

GETHIN   I'm not. Emma's the one trying to out me.

MEGAN   And this Nick character? Is he gay?

GETHIN   Don't think so. Didn't look it.

MEGAN   Funny how most of these gay bars are full of straight people, isn't it?

GETHIN   Jesus. Does it matter? Does it really matter? Why is everyone so interested in my personal life all of a sudden anyway? Didn't think I was that interesting.

MEGAN   If it's not true Gethin, you should set Emma right.

GETHIN   I should, should I?

MEGAN   And if it is, then you've got to...

GETHIN   What would you know about it?

MEGAN   Gethin -

GETHIN   What makes you think you've a right to know what's
               going on in my life...

MEGAN   You can tell me if you're gay.

GETHIN   When yours is such a mystery?

MEGAN   I want to help, Gethin.

GETHIN   Be' ddigwyddodd Megan?
               What happened Megan?

MEGAN   Sshh! Keep your voice down.

GETHIN   Ti'n disugwl i fi weud popeth, a tithe'n gweud dim!
               *You can't expect me to spill everything when you won't
               do the same!*

MEGAN   They're sleeping.

GETHIN   Dechreuais ti pwy noswaith.
               You started the other night.

MEGAN   Gethin -

GETHIN   Did you leave because of David?

MEGAN   David is dead. He died in a car crash.

GETHIN   I know that. Why are you telling me something I already know? I know the story. David died. You left. But it was thirty years ago, Megan. For God's sake! Get over it! Blynydde nol!

MEGAN   Think you know it all, don't you? You hear a couple of stories from your mother and just fill in the blanks yourself. You swan in here with your so-called friends, tear my family to bits, and think you've a right to attack me over something you don't know the first thing about! Because you don't. You don't! *(Beat)* What are you waiting for Gethin? For me to break down in tears? Is that what you want? I wouldn't give you the satisfaction. You're twenty-four. You don't know anything about life except what you see on TV. You hardly understand yourself let alone anyone else. So don't lecture me, Gethin. Don't you dare.

GETHIN   What am I supposed to think? You came out here, and had as little to do with us as possible. Your own father died and you couldn't even be bothered to go back for the funeral. And why? It's pathetic, Megan. Pathetic. I didn't know you until last week. I'd never been in the same country, let alone the same room as you before. So, forgive me for getting it wrong, but what else am I supposed to think, eh?

MEGAN   She didn't tell you how Dad shouted, did she? Didn't tell you they tried to talk me out of marrying him, again and again? Your mother didn't tell you how they made my life a misery because David wasn't like us, because he wasn't Welsh, did she? 'Course not. Because David was English, Gethin, and as far as Dad was concerned that was the worst thing he could be. How could I marry a man who didn't speak his language? A man he couldn't choose his words with? How could I marry a man who was so, different? The traffic was hardly moving. Road works, we thought. I wondered what I'd find when I got back. Dad and David, friends? Or if not friends, at least civil. The bus turned the corner by Rhosyn, and I spotted a police man, ambulance, and a crowd of on-lookers. I could see there'd been an accident, a car spun off the road, down the bank. That's what was holding us up, an accident, and all I could think was, "How can people watch that? How can they stand there and watch that?" *(Beat)* My father was raging when I reached the house. An Englishman would never marry his daughter. Never. I felt sick. Mam couldn't help smiling when she told me how they'd argued. Vicious, she called it. I couldn't stay. But as I opened the door, there was the policeman I'd seen earlier at the side of the road. I knew from the look on his face. I could see his lips getting ready to say sorry.

GETHIN   What about Mum?

MEGAN   I was cold. Numb. I went to the front room to get away, be alone. But I could smell it. I could smell it still in the air. And there was Ruth picking up the half-empty bottle of whisky and screwing on the cap. I saw two glasses on the table. Two glasses. And I could tell she knew, they hadn't even tried to stop him. She knew what they'd done. For days I put up with condolences from the people who'd watched like ghouls as David was cut from the car. Mam, Dad, Ruth created the story in seconds. The roads were wet. He might've been speeding. Behind my back, they were sure he was speeding. A stranger who didn't know the area. English. Killed. *(Beat)* Months later I was here. Australia. Far from home and the lies, the lies I'd choke on if I stayed. It sounds terrible, I know, but I left to hurt them. I wanted them to have bruises too.

GETHIN   Megan...

MEGAN   I don't want to lie anymore, Gethin. I don't want to
               hide anything away. D'you see? We don't have to.
               Come on. What really happened at this gay club?
               You can tell me now.

GETHIN hesitates.

GETHIN   Well, it's just a disco full of boys without their T-
               shirts on, isn't it?

MEGAN   I thought as much.

GETHIN   I didn't mean to upset you Megan.

MEGAN   What you've got to remember is that I like my life
               here Gethin. No, I love it. It's different to anything I
               would've had if I'd stayed. Is it really so hard to
               believe I could be happy?

*MEGAN exits stage left. Pause. Slowly GETHIN walks back to the
sliding doors. He stands in the open doorway. A man comes into view.
GETHIN walks towards him slowly. They kiss. Blackout.*

Act Two - Scene Four

Wednesday. Morning - an unusually bright day. Humour in this scene should be underplayed - as though there is no energy left. The sliding doors are closed. RAY is on stage flicking through a newspaper on the coffee table when RHODRI appears carrying a dry cleaning bag at the glass doors. He tries to open them, realises they are locked, taps on the glass, and RAY opens it for him.

RAY   You'd better get a move on if you want to make it on time, mate.

RHODRI   Yeah, I know. The queue at the cleaner's was unreal. Everyone going in there's trying to find out what the story is with the restaurant next door.

RAY   Why? What's happened?

RHODRI   That Greek place on Military Road. All boarded up, with a cop out front. The bloke in the cleaner's says someone walked in with a pistol late last night demanding money. He'd just started making threats when all of a sudden the CD player kicks in and breaks the silence. The bloke turns round to see what the noise is all about, panics, gun goes off, and runs. Get away car parked around the corner it seems. *(Beat)* Are they still here?

RAY   Yeah, there's a last minute drama going on upstairs. Gethin bought a didgeridoo on George Street yesterday arvo and they're trying to squeeze it into a rucksack that's on the verge of bursting.

RHODRI   God help us.

MEGAN enters.

MEGAN   Rhodri? D'you know what the time is?

RHODRI   Sure. I'm on the way.

RHODRI exits stage-left.

MEGAN   Was that the real estate agent earlier?

RAY   Yeah. Reckons we could have a buyer before the auction if we open the house for inspection next weekend.

MEGAN   The last thing I need right now is strangers traipsing through the place commenting on the furniture.

RAY   Not long now, love. It's almost over. Then we can stop.

CERI, EMMA, and GETHIN, enter stage-left weighed down with luggage. They are bickering.

RAY   Bloody hell guys, have you chartered your own
               jumbo or what then?

EMMA   You collect a fair bit when you've been travelling six-
               months.

RAY   Hope you've gone through those bags one-by-one
               Meeg. Made sure they're not trying to pull a fast one
               with your monogrammed towels.

MEGAN   I couldn't pick one of those up with two hands let
               alone strap it to my back.

CERI   Big shoulders Megan. That's the secret.

MEGAN   Yes well, I'm glad you're not complaining because
               you're about to get something else to carry. A
               memento of your trip.

*MEGAN lifts a carrier bag up from the floor and hands out three
small packages. She scrunches up the bag and puts it in her pocket.*

GETHIN   Thanks Megan.

CERI   Yeah, thank you.

EMMA   Can we open them now?

RAY   Go for your life.

They open their parcels to reveal three stuffed toy kangaroos.

RAY   Just like Christmas Day this, isn't it Meeg?

MEGAN   Something little. To remember your visit.

CERI   Hey! Cheers Megan.

GETHIN   Skippy!

EMMA   Yeah, thanks.

GETHIN makes Skippy noises through his teeth. Everyone looks at him, and he stops.

RAY   Not bad are they? Real 'roo fur and all.

Everyone looks at RAY in disgust.

RAY   Only joking.

RAY moves to the sliding doors.

RAY   Anyway, I hate to rush you, but if you want to make this flight we really should be leaving 'round about, now.

CERI   Yeah, right.

RAY   Soon be home in England, eh? I'll be in the car.

RAY exits.

GETHIN   Well, here we go.

EMMA   Moving out!

GETHIN, CERI and EMMA walk to the doors with the bags.

MEGAN   Are you sure you've got everything?

GETHIN   Think so. Hope so.

They exit. RHODRI enters stage-left dressed smartly in a suit and tie and a pair of trainers.

RHODRI   Well? What d'you reckon?

MEGAN   Very nice. But can I make one suggestion?

RHODRI   You will anyway.

MEGAN   The interview panel might prefer a pair of shoes. Get too close in those and the smell will choke them.

RHODRI   Argh. I knew there was something I'd forget.

RHODRI bounds back off left. CERI and EMMA enter.

EMMA   Just nipping back to make sure we haven't forgotten anything.

MEGAN   Good idea.

EMMA and CERI exit. GWEN enters through the sliding doors.

GWEN   G'day Mum?

MEGAN   Good day Gwen. He won't be long. I've sent him upstairs to put something half-decent on his feet.

GWEN   Right. Still here, are they?

MEGAN   Just about to go. Your Dad's driving them to Mascot. Talking of which I'd better go and make sure he's got money for the car park.

MEGAN exits. CERI enters down the stairs carrying a last item of forgotten clothing.

CERI   Gwen.

GWEN   Mum says you're all packed.

CERI   Yeah. D-day's arrived. How're things?

GWEN   Great. I'm staying with a mate in Surrey Hills.

CERI   Working?

GWEN   Yep. Not acting, but. Remember Blake? Well, he's been trying to start up his own production company for ages, and he's just had the go ahead to make a doco for ABC.

CERI   Nice one.

GWEN   He calls me his PA, but really I just send faxes, answer the phone, and make sure there's coffee in the fridge to feed his addiction. When d'you start on the thesis?

CERI   Next month probably. Soon as I can get my head back into that train of thought. Won't be easy after this trip, mind. Now that I've been to Ramsay Street and seen it for myself I don't know whether it will've killed the magic.

GWEN   They'll never kill Neighbours. There'd be riots on
             the streets of London. And Cardiff.

CERI   Your Mum said the producers of Shellcove had been
             in touch. Did they offer you something?

GWEN   They wanted me to go back and do three days work
             as a ghostly apparition. Monique Stewart comes back
             from her watery grave to tell Melissa that Steven is
             actually Stephanie.

CERI   And you refused?

GWEN   What d'you reckon?

EMMA enters.

GWEN   Anyway, good luck. And you never know, hey?

CERI   No. You never know.

*They go to embrace but notice EMMA. CERI shoots a glance at
EMMA and exits.*

EMMA   Still trying to get your claws into him Gwen?

GWEN   We were just having a talk.

EMMA   Good, because you know after the way you treated him last time, you've got no chance, don't you? You're like shit on his shoe.

GWEN   Jesus, you're a sad cow Emma.

EMMA   Me? I'd've thought you were the sad one after the stunt you pulled the other day.

GWEN   Which just goes to show you shouldn't believe everything you hear then, doesn't it?

EMMA   What?

GWEN   Let me spell it out for you Emma. Imagine this, you might find it difficult, but try anyway. Someone you like, someone you can see yourself falling in love with one day is about to get his head bashed in right in front of your very eyes. What're you going to do about it? *(Pause)* You've forgotten. I'm supposed to be an actress.

RHODRI enters stage-left.

GWEN   Oh and thank you Emma. Thank you for proving what Mum's always said about you Welsh people's right.

EMMA   What's that?

GWEN   You really can't keep your noses out of other people's business, can you? *(Beat)* Ready Rod?

GWEN turns and exits up centre. RHODRI follows.

RHODRI   Yeah.

GETHIN appears at the door. RHODRI stops and turns to speak to Emma.

RHODRI   You can close your mouth now Emma, show's over. *(To Gethin)* Bye, mate.

RHODRI and GETHIN shake hands. RHODRI exits. EMMA is fuming.

EMMA   Did you just hear that? Did you hear what he just said to me?

GETHIN   Emma!

EMMA   What?

GETHIN   I really didn't think it was possible for someone to keep getting it so wrong. Leave it, eh? Please leave it be.

EMMA glares at GETHIN furiously, and exits. GETHIN wanders to the table and collects the wrapped package that is sitting there. MEGAN enters.

MEGAN   Ready?

GETHIN   Almost. I just wanted to give you this. To say thank you. For putting us up, and putting up with us.

MEGAN   You shouldn't've.

GETHIN   I wanted to.

GETHIN gives MEGAN the gift.

GETHIN   What'll you do when the house sells?

MEGAN   Who knows? I wouldn't mind going away for a bit. Hiring a camper and seeing some of the places you've been lucky enough to visit. After all, you should know your own country, shouldn't you?

GETHIN walks towards MEGAN and kisses her on the cheek. GETHIN heads to the door. MEGAN's next line stops him.

MEGAN   Gethin? *(Beat)* Diolch i ti, 'nghariad i.

GETHIN turns and smiles at her.

GETHIN   No worries.

GETHIN exits. Pause. MEGAN unwraps the package - it is a compact disc. She smiles, goes over to the stereo, opens the drawer, and loads it. MEGAN moves away from the stereo and the music starts to play: 'Jive Talkin' by The Bee Gees. MEGAN laughs. The song plays and as she gradually becomes caught up in the music she visibly starts to enjoy it, until she is moving to the music. When the song reaches the instrumental bridge she is at the door looking out towards the driveway. She waves, then lies back against the corner of the wall and enjoys the sunlight which is growing brighter all the time.

At this point music should start to come from the theatre sound system, and cut over the music from the stereo. It gets louder and louder and the lights fade to blackout.

The End.

Caught in the Headlights

Sometimes, driving at night on an Australian highway, you might encounter a kangaroo. If you hit it, you're going to remember it for the rest of your days. Depending on the make and shape of your car, either you, or the kanga, is going to sustain damage.

Don't let this fool you. Most Australians don't see kangaroos on a daily basis. They do not hop down our streets like moose wander through the streets of Canadian cities (or so I've been led to believe).

In this way, kangaroos are like the Welsh playwright in Australia cities. Rarely seen and when caught in our headlights, often blinking, slightly bewildered.

When I first met Roger Williams, he was blinking, slightly bewildered. Surrounded by the Minister for Arts and various other dignitaries, he looked unlike the Welsh mountain man I had expected to encounter. My Welsh stereotype – a version of Tom Jones climbing down from the cliffs speaking/singing some kind of foreign dialect – was caught in the spotlight, and found wanting. Talking to Roger, and eventually working as a Dramaturg on his play, the intricacies and layers of Welsh identity came sharply into focus.

The images of another nation that we carry around in our heads are fed by a host of sources: television, film, fiction, faction, the scrolling through internet sites which pop up when we type in one word – "Wales". In fact, the smorgasbord of junk with which the Internet bombards us reflects the bits and pieces which inform us, on a less-than-daily basis for most areas of the world, about the life of peoples in other countries. Every time we see a riot in Dili, a coalmine closure in the Rhondda, or a flood in Mozambique, we are reminded of our differences: social, economic and cultural. But such news images are just a fraction of the whole. By experiencing a culture and place on a day-to-day basis we begin to see past the sound bites and melodrama of the media frame. Of course, we can't live in every culture on a day-to-day basis.

For the majority of Welsh people, glimpses of Australia are provided by soap operas: *Neighbours, Home and Away* and, in a modern reminder of our colonial past, *Prisoner* (a show well and truly relegated to the dustbin of commercial television in the land of Oz). If you were to believe the world created by Australian soap operas – a world of sun, surf and a neighbourly street so incestuous even Nero would be worried – you might expect America to be overrun with kooky lawyers and hard-core cops, all with bleach-white teeth. We know the fantasy world of such genres is just that – a fantasy. Some of the more "post-modern" versions of US sit-coms have recognised their audiences as smarter than the average bear and allowed a breaking of the naturalistic frame. *Roseanne* started it with post-show chats and *Ally McBeal* continues it with weird, wacky, cartoon moments. Yet Australian television programs continue to sell Australia through "realistic" dramas that offer no commentary on the false and sanitised world they create. Tourism is, in no small part, responsible. Throw in some background shots of the Harbour Bridge and you can sell *Water Rats* to Norway. And Norwegians probably love to believe all Australian cops fly around Sydney Harbour, wielding guns, jumping onto jetties with a light, dramatic "thump".

Of course, more power to the Norwegians. There is no use whingeing about the gap between the reality of the soap-opera world and the one most Australians live in. Television producers are not cultural ambassadors. They have no obligation to break down stereotypes or show the plodding, undramatic lives most of us experience.

What theatre offers, with no obligation to the tourism dollar, is a chance to challenge stereotypes, engage with cultural perceptions, and investigate the life of the Other. *Killing Kangaroos* gives us representations of Australians that both Australian and Welsh audiences can recognise. We see creatures we have seen before: the hassled housewife, the teenage swimmer (with a body worth a Most Popular Newcomer Logie), the slightly-racist-but-with-a-heart-of-gold ocker father, the struggling actress trying desperately to rekindle the fame flame. As the play continues these creatures begin to morph. Their world shows cracks. And, of course, the reason for the break down is the arrival of outsiders –

the Welsh trio whose own make-up of race, gender and sexuality immediately challenges the boundaries of normality surrounding this "typical" Australian family.

While academics have often positioned the Other as a particular race, gender or sexuality we know from our everyday present that the Other is an amalgam of all these factors; a being whose layers of difference overlap, whose "specialness" is a complex intersection of all those things which are different to "us". In the theatre, the physical presence of the actor's body disallows neat categories. We do not see black skin in isolation from the other factors which mark the body – his Nike shoes, her lithe legs. We cannot hear an accent without also seeing the gender which speaks. Otherness is dynamic, inter-acting.

In *Killing Kangaroos,* each side, the Welsh and the Australian, look at one another and make assumptions in relation to Otherness. Each side is attracted and repelled by what they see. Each side has to face their prejudices. The trap Emma falls into is to only see Ceri's black skin and, as such, to assume this is all Rhodri can see. Ironically, she is the one who cannot get past Ceri's racial Otherness.

Ultimately, it is the unearthing of secrets which allows the characters to see each other with new eyes. When the truth – the real reason behind Megan's departure, the real financial situation of the family, the feelings Gethin is trying to surpress – is out in the open, the open suddenly offers more room for them to move, more complex identities for them to inhabit. *Killing Kangaroos* looks the kangaroo square in the eye. Rather than ploughing into it, as if there is a true picture of Australia to be found once the stereotypes have been killed, the play swerves off the road. On this road nothing is as obvious as it originally seemed, nor so easy.

It is through art that we get sustained glimpses of another culture and start to fit the pieces into place. If we're lucky not only do we start to understand the day-to-day lives of those living across the oceans but also those living down the street, and not only on Ramsay Street.

Rachel Hennessy,
Dramaturg, Sydney Theatre Company, October 2000

JAMES WESTAWAY – In Memoriam

I first saw James on stage when he was at the Welsh College of Music and Drama. He was playing the lead in 'Chorus Of Disapproval' and I thought – 'Hello, here's a young, talented, energetic, attractive actor, let's hope he's Welsh!' I was casting my first Made In Wales Season and I needed a young, talented, energetic and attractive actor to play the Jinh in Afshan Malik's 'Safar', and a young Welshman in Sian Evans' 'Little Sister'... Jim was soon in the Company, two days after he left College. In 'New Welsh Drama' he said he found me, initially at any rate, 'scary'. I found him a delight to work with, generous, honest and nearly always enthusiastic, except when it came to warm-ups. He also had more technique than I sometimes gave him credit for, though I never had any doubt about his talent.

James then became one of the founder members of the somewhat unruly extended family that Made In Wales became (at its best) in the late Nineties. Twenty productions plus seemingly endless workshops and playreadings, all followed by voluble sessions in various Cardiff pubs (not always 'The Insole'), created a group that we attempted to glorify with the title 'Associate Artists' of which James and Lowri Mae (who really is scary) were the founder members.

James cared passionately about his art and craft and would talk long into the night about the place of theatre in society, especially Welsh society. He would, however, talk even longer about scenes from favourite films, computers and groups from the sixties and seventies that even I had trouble remembering. He was also a great asset to public workshops with an enviable skill at getting the punters to see it his way despite my best efforts to the contrary. He had them eating out of his hand in Newport!

With Made In Wales he went to Dublin with Roger Williams' 'Gulp' (directed by his old school mate Rebecca Gould), worked on one of our Aberdare projects, played, among many other things, Hitler at Dempsey's and, perhaps best of all, created the part of Sean in Lewis Davies' 'My Piece Of Happiness'. The riveting simplicity and emotional truth of this performance will always stay with me and it was a privilege to watch Jimbo work with Lowri in this show (Dorien, Sharon and David weren't bad either).

On a more personal level, Jim was always a good friend to me, supportive (even when I was playing guitar) though also critical, on one occasion trenchantly so, which I deserved and honour him for. He had his black moments - don't we all - but you knew when James was depressed because you didn't tend to see him. He kept that side pretty much to himself in my experience though there were a couple of occasions when I found him just sitting in my office, not wanting to talk, just sit. Sometimes I gave him a script someone had sent in to read. His comments were always thoughtful, often witty and never as cutting as mine (and he only lost one of them).

My abiding memory of Jimbo (can't remember who first called him that) is of a loping (or was that bouncing?) figure looming up outside the Made In Wales window, pausing briefly to check we weren't having a meeting (we nearly always were) before crashing in and offering to make more coffee. Though, come to think of it, his first entrance on a trapeze through a pyro in 'Safar' is pretty hard to forget as well.

He was a good actor, a good friend and a good man. Thanks Jim, and you can forget the money you owe me...

'Time gives us griefs,
Death takes our joys away'.

Jeff Teare

New Welsh Drama I edited by Jeff Teare and featuring
Safar by Afshan Malik,
Gulp by Roger Williams &
My Piece of Happiness by Lewis Davies is available from
Parthian at www.parthianbooks.co.uk

Cribyn by Sarah Snazell

Sarah Snazell was born in 1965 and brought up in Abergavenny by her mother. As a child she loved to walk in the Black Mountains, which later formed a backdrop to much of her work. In 1984 she went to Newport to do an Art Foundation Diploma, and the following year moved to Leeds to study Fine Art and History. Although she regularly travelled back to Wales, regarding Abergavenny as her spiritual home, she stayed in Leeds with her partner Hugh. She taught art in local colleges as well as her involvement as a local arts organiser and painted at Jacksons Yard studios in Leeds. She completed her MA in 1995, exhibiting in Yorkshire and Wales. In 1996 she won Cymru Ifanc for the first time and was invited to become a member of the Royal Cambrian Academy. In 1998 she was diagnosed with Breast Cancer, and she died the following year.

A longer appreciation of the work of Sarah Snazell can be found in Planet 139, 'Sarah Through the Looking Glass: The Art of Sarah Snazell' by Anne Price-Owen.